Lyla Blake Wa..

# Broadway
# Schrafft's
## and Seeded Rye

### Growing Up Slightly Jewish
### on the Upper West Side

City Publishing
Somers, New York

Published by City Publishing, Somers, NY

Library of Congress Control Number:  2015920620
ISBN- 978-0-692-59901-3 (print)
ISBN- 978-0-692-59904-4 (ebook)

*Editor:* Carol Gaskin
*Book and cover design:* Annette Bensen

# SCHRAFFT'S
## and Seeded Rye

Growing Up Slightly Jewish
on the Upper West Side

*To my oldest and best friend, Suzy,*
*who lived my memories with me from 1st grade on—*
*and to the many, many past and present residents*
*of the Upper West Side whose recollections are*
*an integral part of this book.*

*Historical sketches and unwavering support
provided by Russell Ward,
a fellow Upper Westsider and dearest husband.*

# Contents

༄

# Introduction

Until I started writing this book, I didn't realize what a happy childhood I had. It almost seems impossible that one who never ran barefoot across fields of grass and/or alfalfa could still look back fondly on her youth—days spent shooting marbles across West End Avenue or playing hopscotch on the sometimes sizzling sidewalks of New York City.

Instead of growing up in the Midwest or in a little town in New England, where writers are supposed to grow up, I was born and spent all of my childhood years on the Upper West Side, as it has come to be known. As soon as I saw my first Andy Hardy movie, I realized Broadway, from 72nd to 110th Street, my world, was not Main Street, USA, and our neighborhood did not resemble Carvel, Kansas, or any of the other smalltown neighborhoods depicted so winningly on the silver screen. Not only did we call a high-rise apartment building home, my mother and others eschewed close relationships with those who lived even next door to us. There was no borrowing a cup of sugar; and we certainly didn't walk, nodding to our friends along the way, to church on Sundays—or any other day, for that matter. We were Jewish; and even though the stores observed the "blue laws" and were closed on Sunday, there was a kosher butcher shop that was also closed on Saturday.

Of course everyone wasn't Jewish—it just felt that way. Irish immigrant families lived in brownstones and limestones on side streets that connected West End Avenue, Riverside Drive, and Central Park West, where the mostly upper-middle-class Jews lived in two- or three-bedroom apartments that fit the size of their family. Whatever their lineage, all the children went to school together—P.S. 54 at the corner of 104th Street and Amsterdam Avenue. But after school we lived totally separate lives—and the aura of the neighborhood reflected the Jewish way of life.

On the outside, there were dairy restaurants that served borscht and cheese blintzes, and kosher-style delis, where hot pastrami and knockwurst were available every day of the week; temples and synagogues, mink stoles, and emerald-cut diamonds. On the inside, the kitchen linoleum was scrubbed more than once a day, and the dishes were changed for Passover. Friday night was the traditional family dinner, and more often than not, chicken soup with or without matzo balls was the first course.

In the course of writing this book, I was able to talk to many oldsters like myself who lived in "the hood" during the thirties and forties of the last century. Often he or she would remind me about something I had forgotten—the I-cash-clothes man who walked down the middle of the street offering to buy old clothes; or the Automat that stood on the corner of 104th Street and Broadway; or Levy's Stationary Store at 83rd. While there was not complete agreement on what store was on what block, we did all, to a man or woman, agree: what happened on the Upper West Side didn't stay on the Upper West Side. For most of us, the rules we lived by in our neighborhood were in our bones and traveled with us throughout our lives. Even today, if someone asks me how my family is, and I say, "We're all fine," in honor of my mother I add silently, "Kin a hora," to keep away the evil eye. Assimilated I may be, but there are limits.

The essays in this book are personal essays, my own recollection of what life was like in this very special section of the city—a place where everyone I knew was Jewish, and only the pigeons ate white bread.

# The Upper West Side

In 1899, the Upper West Side didn't exist. Empty fields and farms covered the landscape. The North-South avenues, and the East-West streets existed only on a city planner's map. Only one road connected the future Upper West Side with the rest of New York City. Widened and paved, it was first called Bloomingdale Road, then "The Boulevard" north of Columbus Circle. In 1899, this now much traveled avenue was given the name "Broadway" for its entire length, and that's where our story begins.

The apartment house in which I was born, 375 Riverside Drive, still occupies the southwest corner of 110th street. It was built in 1922, one of the many elevator buildings that sprang up during the housing boom that extended from the late 1800's to around 1930. Riverside Drive developed as a street mainly of luxurious private dwellings—including the Isaac L. Rice Mansion at 89th Street and the Schinasi Mansion, still standing at 107th Street-- and more modest single family homes. The now famous Dakota, completed in 1884 on Central Park West and 72nd Street, was joined by other high rise buildings: the San Remo and later the El Dorado and the Beresford. Central Park West along with West End Avenue, where our family moved in 1939, were preserved as quiet residential streets.

The two other avenues were Columbus Avenue where the presence of the El predestined commercial development, and Amsterdam Avenue where block after block was crowded with low rent housing and small stores. The side streets were mostly row houses, brownstones and limestones, with visible fire escapes mandated by the city to protect the tenants of these low rise buildings.

With the housing boom, and perhaps contributing to it, came the opening of the first NYC underground railway system or subway, built by the Interborough Rapid Transit Company, the IRT, in 1904. It was nine miles long and stretched from City Hall to 145th street with 28 stations. The entrances featured Victorian style kiosks. The fare was 5 cents. rw

# Born Yesterday...
## or the day before

I think the neighborhood we now know as the Upper West Side came into being at around the same time I did—in 1928. High-rise apartment buildings were beginning to crop up along Riverside Drive by then, before the great renovation of the park was even a twinkle in Robert Moses's eye.

My mother gave birth to me at home, 375 Riverside Drive, so she would not have to be separated from her two older children: my brother George (ten) and my sister, June (five). She was a very protective mother. Very. This meant I didn't start school until first grade because my mother thought too many germs lurked in kindergarten classrooms. And when I did go to school, at six years old—the City of New York had the final say here—I trotted off to P.S. 54, one block east on Amsterdam Avenue, bundled up to the chin like Nanook of the North, from September to June. I didn't know what cold air felt like until I was in high school.

Our school didn't have a cafeteria, or even a lunchroom or gymnasium for that matter—I don't know if any other city schools did—so everybody went home for lunch. Some mothers gave their children peanut butter and jelly sandwiches or tuna fish (from a can!). Not my mother. When I got home I would find a hot meal on the table: lamb chops (or possibly calves' liver, which I detested but my mother admired for its iron qualities), a baked potato, and green peas. Often she sat down with me while I ate, maybe to keep me company; more likely to make sure I ate everything on my plate. Anything less was not acceptable. If I overlooked even a pea or two, I would have to live with the guilt of having wasted food that could have gone to the starving children of India. How would it get there? I never asked.

At seven or eight years old, the City, for me, was the block around our apartment house. Without crossing any streets, my friends and I could play hopscotch or jump rope on the sidewalk right outside the door. When we got hot and thirsty from playing, we would go into the corner drugstore with its soda fountain, and try to cajole the soda jerk (sorry, that's what they were called) into giving us a glass of water. This was a step we took only as a last resort when the elevator man had refused to take us up again, having given us three or four rides in the hour before.

I was nine before I was allowed to walk, with my best friend, a few blocks further from home, to 100th Street and Broadway. This was important for two reasons. First, it meant crossing four side streets on our own, and second because on the way we would pass Raymond's Bakery, where even with the limited funds available to a nine-year-old, one could buy a charlotte russe or a linzer tart cookie.

Our new freedom also extended north two blocks to Straus Park, at the intersection of Broadway and West End Avenue at 106th Street. This small area had been named in memory of Isadore and Ida Straus, who went down with the Titanic in 1912. (Isadore Straus was one of the owners of Macy's.) Their names were engraved on a bronze plaque displayed prominently in the park, but we were not interested in history; the smooth, paved paths were perfect for roller skating. We could walk there on our own, skate for hours, and when we fell and skinned our knees, the mercurochrome was only two blocks away.

At ten, my world began to expand. For every block I walked on my own, there were ten blocks behind or forward that I covered with my sister or brother or mother and father, or my teacher when she took us on field trips from school. A favorite destination was the Museum of Natural History, where a huge Tyrannosaurus Rex stood in the Fossil Hall. This was supposed to be a major attraction, and it was for most of the children. Personally, I kept my eyes half closed when we came to the dinosaurs and the mummies—and turned my attention to the many cases of ancient cooking implements wrought by native Indians or Eskimos.

The museum spanned two city blocks, 77th-79th Streets on Central Park West, and in 1935 gave birth to the Hayden Planetarium. Our second-grade class was one of the first to visit the newly opened celestial auditorium, where we learned to identify the planets, the stars, and the constellations. I formed a special relationship with Orion and the Big Dipper, because they were so easy to spot, whereas I never really warmed up to the little splash of stars astronomers had named the Pleiades, or the Seven Sisters.  Frankly I couldn't then, and can't now, tell that splash from any other splash in a star-studded sky.

I knew the City extended way beyond our neighborhood because on hot summer nights, my mother and I would take rides on the Broadway Streetcar, with its open sides that allowed whatever air was stirring to blow gently across the otherwise steamy trolley. We boarded practically in front of our house and rode to the end of the line—42nd Street and 1st Avenue—at which point we stood up, the conductor turned the seats around, and we were facing forward again for the return trip (no additional fare).

On those rides we passed Times Square and its huge billboards: Camel cigarettes—with actual smoke

 coming out of the handsome man's mouth—and the Wrigley's Gum sign, bigger than life, featuring Spearmint Gum, my flavor, in brighter lights than I had ever seen, right up there overlooking the most famous Square in the country. There, too, was the New York Times Building, with the news ticker running around the north side of the building. It was exciting to ride through the theater district—I saw crowds outside the Paramount before Frank Sinatra was old enough to sing there—but at the end of the day we returned to our neighborhood, that one-mile square filled with stores and restaurants, banks and schools, that little piece of Manhattan where I grew up.

# Lincoln
## and
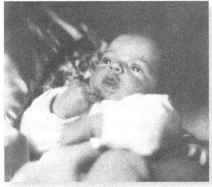

# Me

### Lyla Blake Ward

I've always been grateful to my mother for giving birth to me on February 12th. Family legend has it that she went into labor on the 11th and through sheer strength of character held out until she made sure her youngest, me, would be born on Lincoln's birthday. Legend also has it she thought I would be a boy because she was carrying high, but that's another story.

As soon as I understood what birthdays were all about, I knew there was something special about mine. Otherwise, why would my brother and sister go to school on their birthdays, but stay home on mine? Why would my father go to work on his birthday, but stay home on mine? There was a festive holiday air about the day. Even a five-year-old, or especially a five-year-old, could connect the dots: the citywide celebration was all because of me.

I lost my innocence when I started school and found out—courtesy of my first grade teacher—that it was not my birthday being celebrated by everyone in sight, it was Abraham Lincoln's: the 16th President of the United States. It was in his honor, not mine, the schools in New York City were closed. Although I accepted this new information, I still experienced a little glow each time someone commented on the fact that I was born on Lincoln's birthday. Even before I knew what astrology was I felt a link with this great man, and the more I learned about him, the more convinced I became it wasn't just Chance at work behind the scenes on that snowy day in 1928 when I was born. Destiny had spoken, and I had an obligation to live up to our potential.

Young as I was, I realized I would never bear a physical resemblance to my datemate. Even if I got tall—very tall—I didn't expect to grow a beard, and a stovepipe hat was out of the question. But I liked to think we shared some character strengths. While I could never make my friends refer to me as Honest Lyl, I was always very truthful. If I ate three candy bars an hour before dinner, I admitted it and took the consequences—in my case it meant eating dinner anyway. Someone else, less astronomically blessed, might have been evasive— the clock was broken; I'm just not hungry, I must be coming down with something. Not me. The bar had been set high for me, and I cleared the hurdle.

There were times, I will admit, when sharing a birthday with an iconic figure felt like too great a burden for a short girl whose log cabin was an apartment on

Broadway and 104th Street. On those occasions I had to remind myself that the advantages of having been born on the same day as Mr. Lincoln far outweighed the disadvantages.

First, there was no excuse for anybody forgetting the date of my birthday. Whether it was department store sales or commemorative programs or school plays, February 12th had been long affixed in everybody's mind. My birth only confirmed the importance of the date. As for the birthday celebration itself, I was the envy of all my friends. While other children had to bring cupcakes to school to celebrate their birthdays, I could have my party on the actual date of my birth—a tribute to my predecessor. Unfortunately, my mother, who had gone to such lengths to make sure I was born on the 12th, chose to ignore the circumstances of my birth. And Lincoln or no Lincoln, there were no log-splitting contests at my party. Instead, the table was floating with pink hearts, a positive reminder I was a girl and at best, being elected president of my third-grade class would probably be my greatest political achievement.

To those who scoffed at my pretensions from time to time, I would fall back on the old astrological argument, allowing it was not just Lincoln and me, born on the same date, who exhibited qualities of leadership, concern about humanity, originality, independence, and wit. We Aquarians (January 21st to February 19th) were all known for these characteristics. Perhaps I felt a little more akin to Mr. Lincoln, maybe a little wittier, a little more humane than someone born, say, on February 11th, but no one could deny the scientific basis for our similarities.

That's why I found it particularly disturbing when the claim was made for a thirteenth sign,

Ophiuchus, to be inserted into the astrological calendar, which would, in effect, negate my and Mr. Lincoln's Aquarianism and turn us into practical, prudent, ambitious, disciplined Capricorns.

Luckily, vocal protests against such an unreasonable attempt to change the very roots of astrology won out—at least in newspaper astrological forecasts—and all the hoopla concerning this "new constellation" died down. Future generations will have to fend for themselves, but for now, Abraham Lincoln and I are still considered proud Aquarians.

Since I have never been called on to make momentous decisions regarding the State of the Union, and my storytelling has pretty much been limited to what my children did that day, some might say that the fact that I was born on Lincoln's birthday was not such a big whoopdeedo. I, of course, disagree. I may not be an historic figure, and my profile may not be on any coin of the realm, but on February 12th each year, when the History Channel starts reenacting the Civil War, and schoolchildren in the North recite the Gettysburg Address, as did their sisters and brothers before them, I feel that symbiotic connection taking over, and I have to say, once again, "Thank you, Mom."

# On Reading
## That My Favorite
## Old Wives Tales
## Are Just That

If wet feet do not give us colds,
Or tiny sniffles, even,
And warts are not the work of toads,
What can a gal believe in?

If spinach won't make muscles move,
And milk should not have fat on,
And carrots don't make eyes improve,
What can I hang my hat on?

If iodine can hurt a sore,
And stiff necks don't need bacon,
I'm glad I grew up strong, before
We found we were mistaken.

Good Housekeeping (November '63)

*"Floating Bath" in the Hudson River—1938*
*A no-no for my brother, sister and me*

# Reborn on
# the Fourth of July

I was about seven years old; it was a hot, hot day in June when I first noticed I was the only girl in my class still wearing a woolen skirt. When I reported this to my mother, she carefully explained that other mothers didn't care as much about their children's health as she did, so they allowed them to change into summer clothes, even in some cases go swimming, before we could be absolutely sure summer had come. That was when I learned: official calendar notwithstanding, it was not summer until my mother said it was summer, and in our family, that change of seasons took place on the Fourth of July.

Until then, the shorts, the halters, the bathing suits remained firmly packed away, untouchable until the magic date. Ninety-eight degrees in June? We sweated it out. End of school picnic July 1st? No pleading, no tears could change the rule. My mother was of one mind: protect her young; keep them healthy and safe from the countless perils awaiting us if she did not keep up her vigilance.

Still, even as a child I did not accept dictums without resistance. I didn't want to hear about what could possibly happen to me if there was a sudden change in the weather and I got a "chill." All I knew was, Suzy's mother let her go out to play in her seersuckers when it was "boiling" hot; why couldn't I? Why was mine the only mother in the neighborhood who saw danger around every corner?

I now realize she probably wasn't. Overprotective, she might have been, but looking back, she was not the only parent in the thirties who had a morbid fear of illness; and "chills" were generally accepted as being the dreaded precursor. A child whose body trembled for even a few short minutes might end up (literally) with the grippe, or worse even, influenza, as in the flu epidemic of 1918. To my mother's way of thinking, perspiration would never do us in, whereas if we were caught unaware when a cold wind suddenly stirred, it would lower our resistance, and at the very least we might catch a cold, which even the most careless parents knew could lead to pneumonia.

Adding to the intractability of the family ordinance on changing clothes was the fact that once we had donned our lightweight summer garments, there was no turning back. "Dressing for the weather" was not a tenet my mother subscribed to. She sincerely doubted the body's ability to adjust to changes of temperature. In our house, the woolens were packed away in mothballs on July 5th, not to reappear until after Labor Day weekend, in those years when Labor Day occurred early in September. Otherwise, summer was over when my mother said it was over.

But in the unlikely event one of us did get sick, the greatest of care was taken to make sure that first, we got better, and second, contagion within the family was contained. If there was fever involved, which meant anything above 98.6, and everyone knew oral thermometers were not accurate, you stayed in bed. Over 100 meant a bedpan, because standing on one's feet with a temperature was an invitation to rheumatic fever. To make it out of bed, you had to be normal for twenty-four hours, and to leave the room, because temperatures varied from room to room, you had to be normal for forty-eight hours. I don't remember being out of commission for anything less than a week for even a simple head cold.

As far as the inevitability of one member of the family "catching" a cold, flu, or measles from one another, as is the norm for today's children, the invalid's dishes were kept and washed separately from the rest of the family's and visitation was strictly limited. Of course, Lysol, with its distinctive fragrance, was used liberally on any surface anyone even thought of touching.

After the Fourth or not, pools were never an option. True, with polio still uncontrolled, summer was every parent's nightmare, but I did have friends who swam in the saltwater pools at Jones Beach or even in the corralled areas of the Hudson River and lived to tell the tale. Not me. Either I went in the ocean, when we could get there, or in a lake at summer camp when I was older. To my mother, pools were just contaminated standing water, and chlorine an ineffective irritant. Even in her later years, when home pools were no longer a novelty, she looked at me with undisguised disapproval when I said I was taking my children to swim at a neighbor's pool. Luckily, by age forty I had overcome my fear of contagious diseases and only made sure our lounges were facing east to ward off the evil spirits.

Of course, summer had its counterpart in winter. Here, the temperature outside did dictate our mode of dress. The first day the thermometer dropped below sixty was when the lisle stockings came out of the drawer and our "drawers" became woolies. A mild day in December brought no reprieve. Nature had made its decision, and we were stuck with it.

In all fairness, in those pre-penicillin days, when our doctor's bag of tricks seemed only to consist of aspirin and Seidlitz powders, parents tried to prevent those illnesses for which medicine had not come up with an answer. A woman in her fifties recently told me her mother would line up her and her eight brothers and sisters every morning before school and give them a tablespoon of cod liver oil. It tasted awful, she said, but outside of the ordinary childhood diseases, she doesn't remember any of them ever being sick.

My mother force-fed me calves' liver with spinach on the side to build up my hemoglobin. Luckily for me, she herself did not like black strap molasses, also a great source of iron, so I was spared this daily dose. And occasionally I had to drink malted milkshakes, thought to have miracle nutritional value for thin children. Fish was considered brain food; my mother wanted smart children; ergo we had to face this unpopular meal at least once a week. Because I loved apples, it was no trial for me to eat an apple a day to keep the doctor away, and as long as I peeled the germ-harboring skin, I was free to indulge to my heart's content.

Since I'm writing this at eighty seven years old, one can only conclude that mother was right. She seemed to be years ahead of the "experts" in worrying about food contamination. When I read an article recently saying that E.coli had been found in hamburger meat, I thought how amazing it was that seventy years ago my mother already knew about the dangers lurking in anything chopped up. That's why we were never allowed to eat hamburgers or hotdogs out; not at ballparks, not at street stands, not at Hamburger Heaven. She said butchers ground up odd entrails and other undesirable parts to make the hamburger meat sold in stores. As far as hotdogs went—and they didn't at our house—even Hebrew National was suspect. We

18

answered to a higher power: Mom. Long before chemical fertilizer was used, she washed vegetables and fruit until they shone, then peeled them. I remember her soaking everything before it hit the pot: meats, chickens, fish. When she got finished with a mushroom, it was unrecognizable.

It would be glorifying the past to say her fears have all proven to be justified. If walking barefoot on stone floors adversely affected your kidneys, most of the people in the world would be on dialysis. In some circles, frozen vegetables are thought to be more nutritious than fresh, and nothing has come up to suggest one will die from eating food reheated or even cooked in a microwave.

Fortunately I've gotten past these unproven theories. I do heat water for tea in my microwave and occasionally throw abandon to the winds and eat a potato or two that wasn't fried in Crisco. So what if I do still grind my prime or choice beef at home; want to make something of it? I am definitely not following in my mother's footsteps. I just like the taste better, and besides, it's so easy with a Cuisinart. I don't use her hand grinder anymore.

*P.S. 54 on the corner of 104th Street and Amsterdam Avenue*
*By the time I began school here, in 1934, boys and girls*
*were no longer required to use the separate entrances*
*clearly marked on the building.*

*Broadway, Schrafft's and Seeded Rye*

# Busing

༄

Busing was not an issue when I went to P.S. 54 in New York City. In 1934 everybody walked to public school. Private and parochial schools may have used some kind of car service, but I saw my first yellow school bus many years later, when I moved to the suburbs. We all walked in the thirties and, as far as I know, everybody was still walking when I finished eighth grade in 1942.

Even as first graders, six years old, we walked to school in the morning, walked home for lunch, walked back after lunch, and then home in the afternoon. Four trips a day; rain, sun, or snow. "Snow Days" were not days the school was closed; the school never closed. Snow days were days you got to play in the snow after school. Even though our walk was only two or three blocks, in winter we were bundled up against the weather. We wore snowsuits with ballooning baggy pants or leather leggings to protect our legs against the cold. If it was raining when we left home, we carried umbrellas and wore rubbers on our feet. Someone may have had a raincoat. I didn't. If the rain started after we were in school, my mother and others would be standing outside with galoshes and umbrellas,

*note the wooden desks, perfect for carving initials*

making sure no drops reached us on the short walk home. Occasionally, the rain or snow was so heavy at lunchtime that going home was out of the question. In the event of a real downpour, I remember my mother bringing me lunch in a paper bag and staying with me while I ate at my stained, initial-carved desk in the classroom. (P.S. 54 was the second oldest elementary school in Manhattan, so mine weren't the only initials carved into the wooden top.)

I don't think any of us, in those years, were aware that black children in a neighborhood just ten or twenty blocks north of us were walking to schools even more decrepit than ours, which was no great shakes. The two-story, light-colored stone building on 104th Street and Amsterdam Avenue, dirty even then, had only a few hundred students, kindergarten through 6th grade. The walkers came from the surrounding blocks. Our "integration" consisted of poor Irish-American children, who walked from the streets east of the school, and the middle class, mostly Jewish children, who lived in the apartment houses on West End Avenue or the side streets between Broadway and Riverside Drive. We saw each other in school. After school we went in opposite directions and stayed there until the following day.

Except for rain or snow, we were pretty independent. At seven or eight years of age we walked to school by ourselves, sometimes with a friend or group of children. My best friend lived on West End Avenue on 104th Street. I lived on Broadway. She would pick me up every day and we would walk together, fooling around, sharing secrets, exchanging notes on what had happened in the twelve hours since we had seen each other last. In the morning we walked directly to school, arriving at about ten minutes to nine. We were expected to be in our seats when the bell rang at nine o'clock. We saved our stop at the candy store on the east side of Broadway until the walk home from school at three o'clock.

Our parents didn't worry if we were a little late coming home from school. They knew how wide the variety of penny candy was and how long it could take to choose between a penny's worth of Tootsie Rolls or a licorice stick or a package of bubble gum. Sidebar: Gum was definitely an after-school activity. If a student was caught chewing gum in the classroom, the teacher would order the offender to wear the chewed piece on her forehead the rest of the day as a graphic reminder to the other students of the consequences of civil disobedience.

The only threat to our safety on the streets came around Halloween time, when big kids from the east side of Broadway would come through the neighborhood swinging stockings filled with flour and frightening as well as hurting younger children, who had no place to hide in the solid concrete structures that formed the neighborhood. Otherwise our walk route was secure. A policeman was stationed at each of the two major streets we had to cross: Broadway and Amsterdam Avenue. These were not crossing guards. These were New York City cops, usually on the mature side, who knew many of the children by name and supplemented the traffic lights that flashed red (Stop) and green (Go) when we were supposed to cross. A songwriter of the day, Irving Caesar, put safety rules for children into jingles. The little tune that accompanied "Cross on the Green, not in between" still runs through my mind when I stand on a street corner waiting for the light to change.

Because there were no options, everybody was a

walker, and we didn't consciously think about going to a neighborhood school. We just knew we were going to the school in our neighborhood, as children all over the city were doing. When I see the lines of yellow school buses waiting outside elementary, middle, and high schools today, I feel sad. I think back on my own glorious feeling of freedom, maybe an hour all told in the course of a day, when, my schoolbag swinging at my side, a few pennies in my pocket, I was on my own; just a an ordinary little girl walking two blocks, four times a day, to the school in my neighborhood.

# School Daze

It's hard to tell at seven thirty:
Which face is clean and which is dirty,
Which clothes are soiled,
    and which are ready,
(Are those red stripes,
    or just spaghetti?)
Who likes the roast beef-lettuce-dry,
Who wants the tuna-mayo—rye,
Whose notebook dropped
    between two chairs,
Who left his pencils on the stairs,
Whose hair was washed and
    needs some brushing,
Who dawdles and requires rushing,
Who has a raincoat button missing,
Who's leaving and requires kissing.

Good Housekeeping (February '67)

*"Boys Playing Marbles"*
*Painting by Harry J. Oshiver*

# The Marble Season

The Marble Season officially began when spring sprang forward: Daylight Savings Time. No starting shot was fired. It just happened. On the first mild spring day, children, boys and girls, ranging in age from about seven or eight to maybe twelve or thirteen, emerged from the many apartment houses that lined the side streets between Broadway and Riverside Drive on 104th Street, where I lived. Each of us carried anywhere from one to thirty marbles. Some of us, aspiring entrepreneurs, brought the equipment of our trade: wooden cigar boxes printed with the name "Schulte's," the local cigar store, or cardboard shoeboxes, empty of their I. Miller or Florsheim shoes, with little "doorways" cut out of the sides.

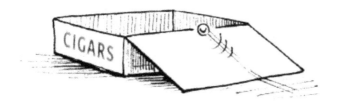

*Step right up*—*5 marbles for every one you get in the box*

The Games were set up on West End Avenue. In the thirties, there was so little traffic we actually shot our marbles right across the avenue. If an occasional car or truck wanted to go through, we stepped back and gave them safe passage. But for the most part, we had exclusive use of the road from gutter to gutter.

It's hard for people who grew up outside the city to picture how very small-town New York neighborhoods were at that time. Our general "community" covered ten blocks, from 106th Street to 96th Street and included Broadway, West End Avenue, and Riverside Drive. In that area, we had two movie theaters, the Riviera and the Riverside; Raymond's Bakery (where the smell of freshly baked cookies greeted you before you even opened the door; Citarella's Fish Market; Shlumbohm's, an old-fashioned ice cream and candy store, renowned for their handmade candy canes at Christmastime; several grocery stores, shoemakers, and butchers; a 5&10: all the services that sustained our comfortable middle-class lives.

Even the most apprehensive mothers (I have a particular one in mind) allowed their single-digit-aged children to go out to play alone with only one caution: "Don't talk to strangers." Otherwise, at six or seven years old we would be allowed to stay on our own block without crossing any streets; at eight we might be allowed to cross one side street, and by the time we were eleven or twelve, we could walk down to 96th Street with a friend or group of friends.

The children who showed up to play marbles were from the neighborhood and stayed as close to home as their ages dictated. I had only to walk the block from Broadway to West End to revel in the carnival-like atmosphere of the seasonal event. And what a season it was.

The weather was mild enough then, not only in the afternoon but in the early evening after a hastily gulped dinner, to begin our play in earnest. Even from the first day, everyone seemed to know the rules of the game. Automatically we divided into two groups: the "businessmen"—boys and girls, we didn't degenderize words then—and the "players." The "businessmen" set up their boxes side by side and attracted "customers" by calling out how many marbles a player could win by rolling his or her marble into the little "windows" or up the cigar box "ramp," or in some cases just by hitting one marble with another. Naturally the further away you stood to shoot, the bigger the challenge, the bigger the pot.

As I got to nine or ten years old, I developed a system. At the beginning of the season, I would take some of the easier shots: rolling my marble from a short distance up a cigar "ramp" or into a "window." The rewards were small but consistent. When I accumulated enough marbles, I would set up "shop," requiring the player to shoot across the avenue into my box or even to hit the one marble I had placed at the curb. I discovered young: the odds are always with the house. Although some of the more skilled or lucky players hit the jackpot, at the end of the day, I was usually the big winner.

It wasn't only how many marbles you accumulated; the kinds and colors were important, too. "Clearies" were always considered quite valuable. These, as the name suggests, were marbles without any swirls of color running through them, just glass, clear or light blue or green or amber. Other marbles were double size. These were prohibited in the games but sometimes given out as prizes. The younger players didn't always realize the value of their marbles, and a "businessman" could wind up with a sizeable collection of "clearies," greatly increasing the worth of her holdings. A good "clearie" could bring as many as eight or ten ordinary marbles and, if business was not so good that day, a trade could provide the necessary capital to carry on.

Outside of playing grocery store and making change, the marble season was my first introduction to business. Although starting out with just a couple of marbles and ending up with a boxful did not prove to be a pattern for my later life, the idea of being in business for myself has always remained appealing. On the other hand, I was on the scene when players lost all their marbles (literally), so as an adult, gambling has never held much attraction for me—particularly roulette. The little ball bouncing around on the numbers reminds me too much of a marble gone wild and, as a former, successful "businessman," I remember how I got all my marbles.

It's been more than seventy years since I shot marbles across West End Avenue or set up my shoebox for others to try their hand at beating the odds. But as soon as the air gets balmy, and the days grow long, and the calendar says it's spring, I smile to myself. It may be spring to my children and my grandchildren. To me it will always be the Marble Season.

# Natural Resources

Children are better at some things than us,

At eating a sandwich and leaving the crust,

At skipping on sidewalks and not touching
cracks,

At reaching mosquito bites down on their
backs,

They're whizzes at loosening a tooth
til it wiggles,

And able to cut up a worm while it wriggles,

Though children, admittedly, may have
their troubles,

They chew gum the longest and make
the best bubbles,

They all have two stomachs, so if one
should hurt

From meat and potatoes, there's room for
dessert,

And what's more amazing, these
marvelous tricks

Most children have mastered before
they are six.

McCall's (November '64)

*2 versions of hopscotch—the smaller the shoe size, the better the hopper.*

# The Sidewalks of New York

❧

If playing is considered the "business" of children, I conducted most of my serious business on the sidewalk that surrounded our apartment house on Broadway and 104th Street. The smooth, hard pavement was perfect for games that required that kind of surface. Starting at about age six, we began mastering our skills in hopscotch, jump rope, hit the penny, and other bouncing ball games, such as one, two, three o'Leary or jacks. These were intensely competitive games, because in each case there was an opponent who might, if allowed, win the game. She might be able to hop better than you could, hit the penny more often than you did, or not get tangled up in the jump rope when trying to remember a name that began with G, as in "G, my name is Greta, my husband's name is George, I come from Georgia, and I sell grapes." One had to have both physical and mental agility to lift one's feet and remember geographical locations at the same time.

My strongest competitor for the title of "jacks queen" was my own mother, who apparently had skipped the chapter in Psychology 101 that said you should let your eight-year-old daughter win. I could hold my own in onesies, twosies, and threesies, but when it came to "cherries in the basket, " my mother was a pro. With her right hand, she would make sure the ball bounced high enough so that while it was in the air, she could carefully pluck a cherry (jack) without touching any of the others around it, drop it in her left hand, and catch the ball easily in her right before it touched the ground again.

Hopscotch, on the other hand, was my tour de force—I was a great hopper. Either I or one of my friends would draw a hopscotch—or potsy, as we sometimes called it—on the pavement with chalk; pretty easy, because the sidewalk was already scored with rectangles outlined with grout. All we had to do was make boxes, numbered one through ten, throw a hard object (we used a skate key) into box #1 (the closest), and then hop into the neighboring box, pick up the key, and hop out without touching a line. The object was to repeat this in each of the ten boxes, with #10 being the farthest away. The first one to successfully hop her way through won the game.

"Hit the penny" was my first gambling experience. For this two-player game, a penny was placed on the sidewalk. The players faced each other, about six feet apart, with the penny in the middle. If you hit the penny you got one point. If you turned it over you got five points. The player who got twenty-five points won the game and kept the penny. In those days of penny candy, winning two games could represent a killing.

Sidewalks were also perfect for roller skating on the four-wheeled roller skates we attached to our sturdy oxford shoes, securing them with the roller skate key that doubled as our hopscotch "object" of choice. These were very stable conveyances—at age five or six. As long as you had the strength to turn the key to put the skates on securely, you were free to go. There were no designated lanes for skating or bicycle riding; it was more a case of pedestrians beware and, since I was the one rolling or riding, it seemed like a pretty fair arrangement to me.

If we wanted to do somersaults or swing on swings, Riverside Drive was only two blocks away. Grass was okay, I guess. But when I took my first trip to the suburbs—my parents had friends who had moved to Yonkers—and I looked around and all I saw were open fields and trees, not a sidewalk in sight, I put my skate key back in my pocket. These kids had no place to play.

# Our Theaters

The Riverside and Riviera Theaters, where I spent much of my childhood, were designed by Thomas W. Lamb and built for the Shubert Brothers in 1912, about twenty-five years before my friends and I settled down in those plushy velvet seats, still plump and unripped, each Saturday afternoon. The ceilings were at least two stories high and elaborately decorated with wood carvings finished in gilt. At the Riverside, there was a painted panel in the dome over the proscenium in which Christopher Columbus seemed to be declaring to Queen Isabella that the earth is round and asking for her help to send him on his way to the West Indies. Michelangelo it wasn't, but the atmosphere was regal, and even the smallest of neighborhood theaters aspired to live up to the description of a movie palace.

The Midtown, the Essex, the Olympia, the Carlton, the Symphony, the Thalia, the Stoddard, the Beacon, RKO 81st Street, Loew's 83rd Street, and of course, the two Rs, were all located on Broadway between 72nd and 110th Street. These multiple movie houses provided screens for the hundreds of films that poured out of the studios, making the Upper West Side, in the thirties, a loving participant in the Golden Age of Hollywood.

rw

# The Moving Pictures

ϛ∿ϑ

If you want to know how important movies were to my
family, consider my given name. Forgoing the traditional
Jewish custom of naming children after a respected
dead relative, my mother, throwing caution to the wind,
named me Lila, for her favorite star of the silent screen:
Lila Lee.

It's not surprising then, that every Saturday, at
nine or ten years old, I was allowed to walk to the Riverside or Riviera Theater, at 95th and 96th Street and
Broadway, where I could watch my screen heroes ply
their trade. Clutching my three-for-ten-cent candies—
Nestle's Crunch, Raisinettes, and a Tootsie Roll—
bought along the way, I would scrunch down in my
seat, sit through a cartoon, a newsreel, and a double
feature, and emerge in the late afternoon, eyes strug-
gling with the light after hours spent in a darkened
theater.

My mother didn't have to worry that anything
untoward was going to happen to her little girl once
I arrived at the theater. New York City had an ordinance
requiring all movie theaters to have a "Children's Section"—a ten- or twelve-row enclosure where girls and
boys up to sixteen years of age were required to sit
under the watchful eye of a Matron, whose job it was to
make sure we didn't escape. This imposing figure, usually of formidable stature, wore a long white jacket over
her clothes, making her easy to spot and not easy to ignore. She carried a flashlight, essential in her line of

work, for discovering who was throwing spitballs at whom, by shining her intrusive light on the suspected culprits.

Naturally, as we got older and were approaching womanhood, at eleven or twelve, the idea of having to sit with "the little kids" became intolerable. So we would stand near the ticket booth, wait for some pleasant-looking couple to come along, ask them to buy tickets for us—which they did more often than not—and walk in with our "parents." After that we were free to sit anywhere we wanted—as long as it wasn't next to a man sitting alone. Young as we were, most of us had had the experience of finding a lone gentleman's hand settled comfortably on one or the other of our knees. We couldn't call the usher; we were illegals, so the situation had to be handled delicately—either with a swift knee-to-chest maneuver as our older sisters had instructed, or, if possible, with a change of seats under cover of darkness.

The movies we saw were all rated MC—Morally Correct. Our parents had no concerns about anything we would see on screen. Hollywood in the thirties played by rules set down by the Hayes Office, an industry-supported censoring agency.

As a result every moving picture was suitable for all ages. Stories were about love and marriage—in that order.

My personal all-time hero was Clark Gable. While Clark (I called him that when we were alone) very often played a womanizer, an adventurer, a gambler, a cad, he was changed by his love for Jean Harlow; Claudette

Colbert; Carole Lombard; Hedy Lamarr; Greta Garbo; Marion Davies; Constance Bennett; Norma Shearer; Helen Hayes . . . and before the movie ended, my man Clark always did the right thing. As did all the other men in my life: Tyrone Power, Errol Flynn, Cary Grant, Henry Fonda. Pirates or princes, there was no hanky-panky—the walls of Jericho came down only after the "I do's" had been said.

The only star that could push Clark Gable aside, in my heart and at the box office, was Shirley Temple, a little girl just one year younger than I was (or so I thought at the time; later, her mother admitted having shaved a year off her daughter's age). Instead of being jealous of this little tap-dancing wonder, I idolized her. Every little girl idolized her, wanted to look like her, dress like her, and be a star. Even I knew that, short of a magic wand, nothing was going to turn my pencil straight, brown/black hair into blonde corkscrew curls. No one was going to mistake me for my golden idol. As close as I could come was to clutch my Shirley Temple doll, play with my Shirley Temple cutouts, wear a bow set at just the right angle, and wait anxiously for the next movie to come out, which, in the early years, could be as soon as three or four months' time.

Between Saturdays we had our movie magazines to keep us in touch. Modern Screen, Photoplay, and Silver Screen fed our insatiable curiosity about the "private" lives and "true" characters of the stars. There were the behind-the-screen stories of which costars of which movies were as much in love off screen as on; or how this or that glamour girl was really a homebody at heart; or why so-and-so couldn't find happiness in her first three, four, or five marriages.

So you can imagine how devastated I was when I learned, courtesy of my brother, who went to Hollywood and worked in the publicity department of one of the major studios, that the "real life" stories I had been devouring for as long as I could read and had ten cents to buy a magazine, were as much fiction as the stories I was seeing on the screen. He, and other young publicists, were paid to make them up without ever having met the stars or even seen them off screen. Luckily I was thirteen before he broke the news to me, and naturally I shared this inside info with everyone I knew.

I have been told the first moving picture I saw was Millie with Helen Twelvetrees. I was three at the time and must confess I don't remember much about it. The story, as I later read, dealt with a woman who has several unhappy marriages, swears off men, and ends up shooting her former suitor because he is making love to her sixteen-year-old daughter. Aside from the happy ending (she's acquitted), it seems an unlikely choice for a three-year-old, but since I had no idea what was going on, the only effect it had was to make me a lifelong aficionado of film. Well, maybe that's a little grandiose. Let's just say, nothing much has changed in the way I feel about going to the movies: it was and is the ultimate treat. Substitute night for day; popcorn for candy; and Meryl Streep for Shirley Temple, and I'm here to tell you: when I am at the movies, I am in pig heaven. (Not to worry—we were never Kosher.)

# Growing Up Slightly Jewish

ॐ

I may not have gone to Sunday School, but I always knew I was Jewish. I hadn't even heard the phrase "conflicting messages" until my children, who did go to Sunday School, told me that's what I had sent them.

Apparently eating matzo sandwiches during Passover and chocolate bunnies on Easter was confusing to young girls who, unlike me, had grown up with Catholic friends, Protestant friends, and Jewish friends, most of whom stuck pretty closely to the doctrines of their faith, or their family's faith. Even if the term "identity crisis" had been bandied about in the 1930s, I don't think I would have had one, because in our neighborhood, being Jewish was a given—how Jewish was something else.

There was a family in our house on 104th Street who were so orthodox, they asked the elevator man, Lennie, to come into their apartment on Friday night and turn on the electric lights; they were not permitted to turn on the lights or the stove or any other appliance during the Sabbath. It was also rumored they tore up sheets of toilet paper before sunset on Friday, because religious law prohibited cutting or tearing from sundown Friday to sundown Saturday. I did not personally long to be part of such orthodoxy, but I respected and was a little in awe of their holiness.

Although my sister and I exchanged Fannie Farmer Easter eggs—chocolate on the outside, yellow and white on the inside—each and every year, we also went to temple with our parents on the High Holy Days. That is, we walked with them to Temple Ansche Chesed at 100th Street and West End Avenue. We didn't actually go inside—not right away; we didn't have our own tickets. The way it worked was: prospective congregants were given the opportunity to buy tickets—reserved seats—to services on Rosh Hashanah and Yom Kippur. The seats were sold in much the same way as tickets for a Broadway show: you paid more for the seats down front than for those toward the back of the "house." Seats were pricey for those times; the Depression lingered. So most parents bought just two tickets with the understanding that, when seats on either side of theirs became vacant (congregants went in and out of temple all day) the children could occupy those seats until the true owners returned, at which time we were unceremoniously asked to leave.

If there was a spiritual thread that ran through the services, I never caught it. The prayer book, which I also borrowed from whoever seat I was sitting in, was mostly in Hebrew, and that was the book from which the rabbi read. I did enjoy the cantor's songs. If I was lucky enough to be in a seat when he sang Ein Keloheinu, I would join in for the title words and hum the rest with some lip movement I thought might fool anybody who happened to be looking into thinking I was fluent in Hebrew. For one or two days a year, I regretted not going to Sunday School. And then it passed

In the afternoon, usually at about three o'clock, the doors of the temple swung open and even those who did not have regular tickets could find a vacant seat and join their fellow supplicants in reciting the Mourner's Kaddish, a prayer for the dead. Since children and those who had not suffered a loss were not expected to attend Yis Ga services—and we didn't—I imagined, and nobody told me otherwise, that when the grieving grownups were led into the sanctum sanctorum, a dark and mysterious ritual took place, causing them to emerge, as did my mother and aunts, with somber faces and red eyes. Although I was relieved that they did come out and looked at me with their, you-shouldn't-know-from-this half-smiles, it only confirmed my growing uneasiness about Judaism: this was not a happy religion.

But the darkness lifted when it came to clothes. Everybody dressed up for the holidays. Nothing in the Jewish faith said a woman could not look her best while atoning for her sins. So those who could afford the latest fall fashions wore them. It was not unusual to see a Sally Victor hat, or even a Lilly Dache, atop the head of a prime ticket holder, and though too early for full-length mink coats, silver blue mink stoles or fur scarves complete with the heads and tails of stone martens or sables were worn over trim custom-made suits or fine silk dresses. I don't remember what fur my mother had before she got her mink stole, but I do remember those lustrous, silvery skins she wore proudly to herald in the Jewish New Year.

The children looked pretty spiffy, too. The boys wore shirts, ties, and jackets, which didn't always stop them from roughhousing, ending up with their pre-tied bow ties slightly to the left of center. My friends and I wore new Mary Janes each year, until, like our older sisters, we graduated into low-heeled pumps and clothes befitting girls who were now in high school. When the shofar sounded at sundown, marking the end of the Holy Day and the beginning of the Jewish New Year, there was a feeling of relief: we could all go home now, and those who had fasted could break their fast with orange juice and smoked fish. We had been forgiven for our sins—the slate was clean. By the time we got home, the tiny flames in the yahrzeit candles had gone out; the mourning was over.

Maybe because I didn't know I was getting mixed messages, I never felt conflicted about eating matzohs on Passover and jelly beans on Easter, and because I had only one friend who didn't have presents to open on Christmas morning, I assumed this festive season was for everyone. As far as I knew, Santa Claus didn't discriminate. When his float appeared at the end of the Macy's Thanksgiving Day Parade, sled piled high with gifts, he waved to all of us children, and I never doubted he would find his way to our house on Christmas Eve. And to this day I'm still grateful that my parents didn't block the fireplace.

# Jewish Superstitions

Throughout the ages, most cultures around the world have passed down superstitions from generation to generation. Who hasn't shivered a little when a black cat crosses her path? Does anyone go out of his way to walk under a ladder? Jews, while accepting the general cautions of all societies, have a special list of advisories meant to protect followers of the faith. Here are eight of the most popular.

&ast; If you open an umbrella in the house, it will rain on your wedding day.

&ast; When you move into a new house or apartment, make sure you have salt, sugar, a loaf of bread, and a broom.

&ast; Before wearing new clothes, put a small amount of salt in the pockets to keep away any demons that may be hiding in the dark recesses.

&ast; A pregnant woman should not go to a cemetery.

&ast; Under no circumstances should you have a baby shower or have baby clothes or baby furniture delivered before the baby is born.

&ast; To ensure a safe trip, before embarking, place a pin out of sight on your clothing.

&ast; Never eat a single olive. Two are social—one is eaten only after a funeral.

&ast; Tie a red ribbon on your infant's crib to protect her/him from any evil spirits that may be in the neighborhood.

rw

# You're Looking Well---
# Kina Hora

I was setting the table for Thanksgiving and asked my mother how many places to set. She answered. "Fourteen." As I started to count off the names, assigning a number to each as I went along—"One, Aunt Mattie, two Aunt Marguerite, three Uncle—" my mother shouted from the kitchen—"No—no— never count the people at a table—God forbid, next year one of them will be missing." I knew what "missing' meant—dead.-- and that was the end of my counting people around a table—ever. If Uncle Joe was going to die it wasn't going to be on me.

This was the first time I heard this particular superstition, but by the time I was nine or ten, I had been exposed to a lot of mythology—very little of which was Greek. If the hem of my skirt came down, and I wanted my mother to sew it up while I was still wearing it, she would only sew if I chewed on a piece of thread. I knew better than to ask why, I just took the piece of thread and started chewing.

Some mothers I heard about did the "pooh, pooh, pooh" thing, symbolically spitting three times after hearing bad news or even good. My mom was more into kina horas.* This was almost the same as protective spitting, but with a more positive twist.

** *kina hora is the colloquial pronunciation for kein ayin hora 'which roughly translated means 'may the evil eye stay away'.*

You meet someone on the street—she looks spectacular; tanned, slim, healthy—and you say, "Oh Jane—you look great!" If you're not Jewish you may leave it at that—a nice compliment and move on. In our circle, if this kind of remark is not immediately followed by a kina hora, the receiver of the compliment is doomed. As a child, I was not quite sure how this worked, say in the case of Jane: if the complimenter forgot to say "kina hora," would the woman become pale, fat, and come down with some dread disease on the spot? Or at some future time, would you hear that Jane had completely lost her looks and her health?

For most things I took my mother's word. Without going into the specifics: bad things will happen if you open an umbrella in the house; if you put your shoes on a dresser or a table; if you have a layette delivered before the baby is born. But the day someone stepped over my legs when I was lying on the floor in gym, I became a true believer. I had been warned never to let anyone step over my legs—if I did, my growth would be stunted. I was a little skeptical until one fateful day, when I was twelve years old and the tallest girl in my sixth grade class. The gym teacher told us to lie on the floor and start doing leg raises. I hadn't been down for more than a couple of minutes when Dorothy Gold decided she wanted to be on the other side of me, got up, and stepped over my legs before I could stop her. The deed was done, and from that day on, I went from being the tallest girl in the class to the third from the shortest. What can I tell you?

I took most of the admonitions with a grain of salt (which I immediately threw over my shoulder). I knew my mother was just trying to protect me, in the same way she cautioned me to cross on the green not in between, or not to take candy from a stranger. She never exactly spelled out what would happen in those instances either—she didn't have to. I got the message over and over again. After all, I was a sturdy, bright, happy little girl, and if she had her way, I was going to stay that way—God willing, kina hora, pooh pooh pooh—whatever it took.

# History of the Fur Business

The fur district, stretched from 28th Street to 34th Street on both sides of Seventh Avenue. Most of the furriers had immigrated from Eastern Europe and Russia bringing their skills with them. At one time there were more than 800 furriers in this small area, Business was booming.

If you lived on the Upper West Side chances are you knew someone in the business--an uncle, a cousin, a friend--so when the time came to buy a Persian, a beaver, a mink, you would know just where to go. Still, acquiring a coat would require a significant amount of money and a lot of time because coats were almost always custom made and the process was both painstaking and time-consuming.

The first thing the customer had to do was decide on the style. There were a wide variety of offerings—The furrier would being out samples of coats, either in muslin or fur, that had collars that stood up or lay flat, sleeves that were flouncy or more subdued, bodies that were full or bodies that were slim and fitted. Once the customer had "designed" her coat, and she had chosen an arm from here and a body from there, down to the buttons, if there were to be any, she was presented with a bundle of pelts, in the case of mink—male or female—and she would decide, on the basis of color, luster, weight, the skins she wanted to be her coat. Since the pelts from more than one animal were involved only a highly skilled employee called a "nailer" could actually create the desired fur.

Skins chosen, the customer's measurements were taken--arm length, waist and chest dimensions, height. These would be used to make a muslin pattern, and it was to this pattern any adjustments would be made. Two fur fittings, several weeks apart, followed, and then came the final step—choosing the lining. For those not lucky enough to know someone who could "get it for you wholesale" there were also the retail furriers like Russeks or Jay Thorpe.

rw

# Keeping Up With
# the Cohnses

∽

I didn't get my first fur coat until Christmas the year
I was sixteen years old, but that doesn't mean I was un-
schooled in the characteristics, quality, and appearance
of all the little furry animals whose skins adorned the
ladies of the Upper West Side. I knew when a sheared
beaver was not evenly sheared or when the curl on a
Persian lamb was not tight enough. I also knew that
beavers, lambs, and nutrias were just furs-in-waiting, to
be replaced, hopefully in the not too distant future, by
the number-one arbiter of social status, mink. It was
this little animal, worked into coats, jackets, capes, or
stoles, that was undoubtedly the most svelte pelt—a fur
that announced to the world, or at least to the neighborhood, the wearer's husband was doing extremely well—
extremely well.

Of course it couldn't just be any old mink—
color was a dead, you should pardon the expression,
giveaway. Dying minks—that is, changing their natural
color—was not yet a widespread practice in the thirties.
A "good" mink was dark brown, but not too dark; with
lustrous pelts, narrow, but not too narrow (2-1/8 inches
was about right); and lined with an embroidered or tex-
tured pure silk; striped or plain satin; or crepe, with the
owner's initials hand-sewn on one side.

Many of the linings were chosen from the
bolts of luxurious fabrics imported and stocked by

D. Freid & Sons, whose impressive clock stood on the corner of 32nd Street and 8th Avenue until the blocks around Penn Station were "gentrified." My best friend Suzy's grandfather was the D in D. Freid & Sons, and her father was one of the sons, who, at the time of my material awakening, ran the store. By the time I met Suzy in first grade, she was already on her third fur coat, courtesy of her grandfather David. Until her grandfather died when she was nine, she received whole coats of squirrel, fitch, or summer ermine (stepsister of the royal white), which set her aside from the rest of us third- and fourth-graders who had to make do with cloth coats only trimmed in fur—collars and sometimes matching cuffs. Grey Persian lamb was a favorite.

I would have preferred the foxes that were beginning to adorn my mother's and sister's clothes. Not to be outdone by Greta Garbo or Irene Dunne or other

beauties of the Silver Screen, my mother's friends, and soon my sister's, were beginning to be swathed in fox—silver fox, gray fox, white fox framed their faces—and how I would have loved to have them frame mine. By the time I was old enough to wear them, I was also old enough to recognize that, at my five-foot-three height, had I been swathed in fox, with my small head poking out from the luxuriant folds of the fur, I might have been mistaken for the fox herself.

Like others of my generation, my consciousness had not yet been raised in regard to the killing of animals for fashion indulgence, and while the foxes had nothing to fear from me, if someone had offered me a leopard hat, or a beaver muff, or an ermine cape, or a stone marten scarf, or a sable anything, I would have said "Thank you" and not lost any sleep over the poor creatures, who, I now know, didn't ask to be a muff or a hat or a scarf. Didn't we see Eskimos, year after year, in our geography books, wearing sealskin jackets—even pants? And weren't they admired for their oneness-with-nature culture?

That's why, when I received my gift of fur, a full-length black Persian lamb coat—small curls tightly wound—from my parents, I didn't question the origin of the species or whether the lambs had gotten a fair trial. All I knew was: Suzy and I were now on an equal footing; it was a cold, cold winter; and I loved my new-found warmth.

*Our first set came in a gold toned box with faux ivory houses and hotels and especially lovely "Get Out of Jail FREE" cards.*

# This Machine Accepts Slugs

Not everybody has a real live pinball machine in their apartment. We did. I must have been about nine or ten—we were living at 470 West End Avenue at 83rd Street at the time, and since we did not have live-in help, the "maid's room" was empty. One day when I got home from school, on my way to the kitchen for my afternoon snack, I noticed a big boxy object, all lit up, sitting smack in the corner of the small room that was right off the entrance to the kitchen.

It didn't take long to realize I was looking at a pinball machine just like the one I had been playing since I was four or five years old whenever we went to our family's favorite hotel in the Catskills. It seems almost indecent now—a father teaching his little girl how to use a pinball machine—but in the 1930s the sight of a child putting a nickel in the slot, pulling the plunger back, and sending the little steel ball spinning on a machine would not have rated a second look from any of the other guests, particularly since the pinball machines were not close to the rocking chairs on the front porch.

I wasn't particularly adept at aiming the ball, but every so often, through no skill of my own, the little steel ball would hit its target and I was a winner. Most of the nickels I had played were returned to me, and I was set for another hour of innocent gambling.

That's why it was so exciting to find our very own pinball machine sitting in our very own house to be played whenever we wanted. The only difference was that if we won on the hotel's machines, nickels—lots of nickels—came pouring out. In our machine we were only allowed to use slugs, so even the grand prize had no monetary value; no one in the family was willing to exchange a fistful of slugs for even half a fistful of nickels. Still, it was good practice for my future casino visits, and my friends loved coming over to play, because while we could play ordinary "house" at anybody's house, at mine we would pit Shirley Temple against Flossy Flirt and see which doll could win more slugs.

The resorts we stayed in in the late thirties didn't have casinos per se, but in addition to pinball machines, slot machines—many accepted pennies and paid out in kind—were placed strategically in corridors or game rooms, alongside ping pong and billiard tables. No skill was required to play the slot machines, just enough strength to pull down the lever. By the time I was eight, I could play the slots along with the best of them, and the prospect of seeing three cherries appear on the screen, which happened every so often, was enough to keep me going until the dinner gong rang.

With my early introduction to horse racing (see My Father, the Director) and games of chance, I was addicted to gambling by the time I was ten. Luckily for me, in 1935 Parker Brothers introduced Monopoly, a board game that broadened my financial horizons. Here I could wheel and deal, buy and sell real estate, praying I would land on both Boardwalk and Park Place before they had been bought by someone else. Now, instead of pennies and nickels, I was dealing in tens and twenties and hundreds. I would even keep a five-hundred-dollar bill stashed under my ones to fool my opponents into thinking I didn't have enough money to build a house or a hotel if I got a monopoly. Sure, it was fake money— what of it? It still gave me the chance to gamble on my own ability to prevail, and taught me a valuable life lesson. Even though it was only small change I was using, if I lost my pennies or nickels, I was losing real money; whereas if I should happen to drop a few thou in Monopoly, it was only a paper loss. Nobody got hurt; I would still collect my $200 when I passed "Go;" and I probably could get at least $50 for my "Get out of Jail FREE" card, and come out smelling like a rose.

# History of Brunch

The word "brunch"—that playful blend of "breakfast" and "lunch"— first appeared in print in an 1895 Hunter's Weekly article. In "Brunch: A Plea," British author Guy Beringer suggested an alternative:

"Instead of England's early Sunday dinner, a postchurch ordeal of heavy meats and savory pies, why not a new meal, served around noon, that starts with tea or coffee, marmalade and other breakfast fixtures before moving along to the heavier fare? By eliminating the need to get up early on Sunday, brunch would make life brighter for Saturday-night carousers. It would promote human happiness in other ways as well. Brunch is cheerful, sociable and inciting. It is talk-compelling. It puts you in a good temper, it makes you satisfied with yourself and your fellow beings, it sweeps away the worries and cobwebs of the week."

— William Grimes, "At Brunch, The More Bizarre
The Better" New York Times, 1998 [7]

According to Farha Ternikar, the sociologist and author of Brunch: A History, it was in 1896, when the tradition of a weekend not-quite-lunch made landfall in New York. Its antecedents dated back to the United Kingdom and the "hunt breakfast," where servants would prepare a day's catch after the hunting party returned, resulting in a later-than-usual eating time.

Speaking to an audience at Manhattan's New School at an event coordinated by the Culinary Historians of New York, Ternikar explained that brunch had been around for more than two decades by the time Prohibition went into effect in 1920. Brunch didn't really take off until the wealthy—i.e., those who still had access to alcohol and the freedom to imbibe without fear of repercussions—began using it as an opportunity to day drink, inaugurating the time-honored custom of washing down French toast with mimosas and Bloody Marys.                                     rw

# Brunch at Home

∽

As a child I felt stigmatized by the fact that we had brunch on Sunday. My friends ate breakfast, lunch, and dinner on the weekends, just as they did on weekdays. Maybe breakfast was a little later than usual, but they didn't skip one meal altogether and use a fancy, new-on-the-scene name to describe the two that had been scrunched together. It was humiliating.

I didn't object to the reason we had this contracted meal; I liked sleeping late on Sundays. It was just that I was the only one in my immediate circle of eight-year-olds who was encouraged to get up whenever she wanted to. Only my mother would say, "You need your rest," and make bacon and eggs whenever we drifted into the kitchen.

Actually it was my father who made the bacon, stretching each slice out to its full length and carefully turning it over and over again until it was lightly browned on each side. I mention this because, to my knowledge, bacon was one of only two foods my father ever cooked. The other was a boiled egg. Somewhere along the line, he had learned how to put water in a small saucepan, bring the water to a boil, add the egg, and cook it for exactly three minutes from the time the water started to boil again. He would time it with his stopwatch, which was almost an appendage of his person, and then put his three-minute egg in an egg cup—a tiny ceramic dish with a hollowed-out oval perfectly shaped to hold one egg.

Skillfully slicing off the top of the egg, he would eat the rest out of its own shell. This, however, was only a weekday egg. To go with our bacon on Sundays, our eggs were scrambled or sunny-side-up, courtesy of Mom. A cinnamon bun or other freshly baked coffeecake finished off our unorthodox meal.

Not too hard to take, even for a traditionalist like myself, but having brunch, instead of breakfast and lunch, was only one of many ways our family disappointed me. I desperately wanted to have cousins—first cousins, second cousins, third cousins—who came to visit on Sundays or to whose houses we would go to celebrate birthdays, anniversaries, holidays. Long before the atom was split, ours was a nuclear family. Or at least we acted like one.

My mother was actually from a large family— four brothers and four sisters, of whom she was the youngest. The boys all moved to the Midwest as young men and had families we only met once or twice in our lives. Two of the sisters never had children, and the one who did was completely alienated from the rest of the family. So while my friends were going to family circle meetings where "the cousins" played games and reveled in their kinship, I was looking for another disassociated child to play with on Sundays after my sister had tired of designing clothes for my paper dolls.

To my shame, what my father did for a living also set us apart. If he had been thinking of his future family, he would have been a furrier or a cloak-and-suiter, like all my friends' fathers were. But no—my Dad had to be in the motion picture business. His occupation didn't show much on the outside—that is, he looked like everybody else's father: five-nine-ish, slightly balding, tending toward the corpulent. He wore a felt hat, a suit, tie, and shirt even on weekends. And his work schedule was pretty normal: he started work at nine and was home by six o'clock most days. But he seemed to be the only man on the block who was not in some way connected to Seventh Avenue.

Though no one in my family ever got into the nitty-gritty of their childhood or discussed age, there were veiled references to the fact that my father was about twelve years old when he started working, sweeping out theaters in uptown New York City. So he was in on the ground floor, so to speak, when movies appeared on the scene. He must have been in school long enough to learn to read—and read well—because throughout his life he read two newspapers a day from first page to last and was able to read and understand the fine print in the many contracts that came his way as he emerged from the dustbin and began his career as a director and producer of short subjects, most of which were released through Columbia Pictures. By the time we met, he was already well established in this offbeat profession that so embarrassed his youngest child.

Our casual Sunday schedule had at least one advantage, or what seemed like an advantage at the time: neither my sister nor I ever went to Sunday School—it started too early. As a result I grew up with a very hazy idea of what Judaism was all about. I ate matzos during the eight days of Passover, even religiously making matzo sandwiches to take to school during the week, but I had no idea why I was doing it. It just made me feel very virtuous, like fasting on Yom Kippur, or at least not eating anything I liked that day. In this respect our family was not too different than others in our neighborhood. Although some children went to religious school, many, particularly girls, did not. My brother had been a Bar Mitzvah (he must have gone to night school) and had the obligatory fountain pen to show for it, but when I was eight, he was eighteen, and by that time my parents apparently felt, having given a son to the religion, the girls would benefit more from an extra hour of sleep.

As far as my friends were concerned: my father was an orphan (he wasn't); and my mother's family lived in a place called Cleveland, three thousand miles away; otherwise our many relatives would have been happy to visit us on Sundays. And the brunch? This was harder to explain away. Well, we had brunch because— Anyone wanna play jacks?

# Camp Sight

The list for campers really hurts:
Ten pairs of shorts,
    ten short-sleeved shirts,
Three pairs of jeans,
    three bathing suits,
Some sneakers, shoes,
    and riding boots,
A lightweight sweater, plus a jacket,
A fishing rod and tennis racket,
Some shirts and shorts in tennis white,
A sleeping bag, canteen, flashlight,
A pad, a book of stamps, a pen,
To make sure he will write you when
He gets to camp—then you will read,
"Dear Mom, Love camp.
    Here's what I need—"

McCall's '67

*Broadway, Schrafft's and Seeded Rye*

# Straight Genes

When I was a child at summer camp, about seven or eight, Miss Minna used to come once a week to shampoo our hair. She looked rather delicate and rarely spoke, but when she started to rub the plain Castile Soap into your scalp you felt as if you were being attacked by ten hammers with steely heads. "Shampoo Day" was a day to be dreaded.

My hair, unbraided, fell almost to my waist. Electric hairdryers not being part of the equipment of the day, drying was done by hand and air. After Miss Minna had fine-combed my wet, tangled locks (a painful process only one who has experienced the unique torture of this tiny toothed instrument can understand), she would towel-dry it, with that same extraordinary vigor. Then I would be told to sit in the sun along with any other girl foolish enough not to have had her hair cut before the summer. I think that might have been the time I had my first inkling that hair was going to play an important role in my life, first as a girl child then as a woman.

At that early age I was proud of my long hair, and on those rare occasions when I was allowed to wear it "loose," for a party or my birthday, I felt pretty special. A friend of my mother's used to have exquisite bows made to match each of her outfits. One day, as a gift, she gave me a box of bows in a medley of patterns and colors. The box had a celluloid insert on the cover, so you could immediately see the profusion of color inside. With my new wealth, I, too, had a special bow for each outfit. The fact that my hair was bone straight was neither here nor there. The important thing was: my hair was longer than anyone else's; I had beautiful bows; and when it came to playing "Rapunzel" I always got the title role.

I lived in this world, where length was strength, until I was about twelve. At that time the powers that be, my mother and older sister, decided I wanted a haircut. With womanhood rapidly approaching, they said, I needed a "style." That's when the emphasis shifted. Long straight hair was an attribute; short straight hair was a handicap, a "condition" requiring treatment. I had to have curls, they said, and since my cut hair showed no signs of making them on its own, the answer was a "permanent wave."

I think the price was $10. My memory's a little fuzzy on that point. But I do remember clearly what get-

ting a "permanent" was like in those days. Naturally, you sat on an adjustable barber's chair, like all the other ladies, with a cotton cloak covering you from neck to toe. The hairdresser would take tiny portions of hair, one by one, wet each down with a "permanent" solution, then wrap what I remember as a piece of tissue paper around the strand before rolling the hair on a very thin curler. When your head was completely covered with these little packages and all the hair taken up, a stand with many cords dangling from it was wheeled up to your chair, and each little curler was attached to one of these electrical cords. At that point the beautician turned on the switch, and your hair began to cook. The process was not too much more appealing than Miss Minna's shampoos, but the result, of course, was curly hair—very curly hair.

At first, I was dazed by the change in my appearance. It took a while for me to know who I was looking at in the mirror. But gradually, the magic of the curls took over. I couldn't stop tossing my head around and watching the ringlets stay together. Amazing. Unfortunately, the perm had a limited lifespan. When my hair began to "grow out," and each haircut resulted in fewer curls left on my head, I remembered the torture of the "treatment" and resisted being repermed. It was not that I was going "straight"—by then I was a devout curl convert—I just decided to try curlers instead.

These were the early for-ties. Curlers were small metal tubes, not too different than the ones used for "permanents," around which one wound one's hair tightly enough to be painful and secured each with a metal bar  that was attached at one end. The victim wore these to bed at night, so that when she woke up in the morning (at twelve years old I would have slept even if the pillow had iron spikes) her head was covered with horizontal Shirley Temple curls.

I became very attached to my curls. I set my hair every night, and when I combed it out in the morning, I thought I looked, as we would have said then, like the cat's pajamas. Almost-black, curly hair to the shoulders. Not too terrible. Unless it rained. Then I would start out in the morning with ringlets framing my anxious thirteen-year-old face and return, mortified, with straight, frizzy hair standing a good distance out from my head. Even if the air was only slightly humid or rain was expected in the next county, one by one my curls unraveled. This might not have been so bad if my best friend did not have naturally curly hair that rain and humidity only made curlier. She said she would have preferred straight hair, but then she was my best friend.

Although some things improved as I grew up—metal curlers gave way to rubber curlers that were a little softer than their forbears, and eventually hair rollers, even less painful—my hair "problem" was ever present. I would go swimming curly and come out straight. Unfortunately, the magazines available at the time (SEVENTEEN came out when I was seventeen) showed page after page of young models and movie stars with undulating hair, ranging from deep wavy to softly curled. Not a straight-haired head among them. Editors at the time felt no compulsion to emphasize diversity. In my innocence, I thought all these young women had been born blessed with waves, and each month as the new issues appeared, I was sure there was only one kind of hair to have, and I didn't have it.

Other pleasant features notwithstanding, a girl whose hair hung dankly at the mere sign of drizzle could not hope to attract a young man, even one with straight hair himself. (In those days a boy's hair was not an issue.) Or if it happened, and they met on a curly day, how would he feel starting out with Shirley Temple and ending up with Jane Withers?

As I got older, and began going to the beauty parlor on a regular basis, hairdressers would always tell me what good quality my hair was and admire its color—brown, almost black. That was as comforting as having a boy tell you what a great personality you have. From time to time when I felt I had worn one "pageboy" too many, I would have a perm. One year it was a Kit Kat Kut, another time it was a Poodle, but basically I kept the curler industry in business and relied on "sets" to keep my ends turned under until many years later, when life handed me a lemon.

Following a bout with cancer (thirty plus years ago—knock on wood, spit, spit, spit) I had a course of chemotherapy and lost not all, but a lot of hair. And while I wouldn't recommend this as a beauty treatment, here's where the lemonade comes in. When it was over, not only did my hair grow back, dark and even fuller than before, but wonder of wonders, it grew back curly: not frizzy, not wavy—curly. After rain—curly. After humidity—curly. Nobody knows how it happened or why, and I can't legitimately claim credit for making the lemonade, but I will tell you this. When I come out of the shower and comb my hair into a natural "pageboy," this is not Miss Minna's little girl. This is one happy camper.

# Savings Banks

My mother's East River Savings Bank was prominently located on the northwestern corner of Amsterdam Avenue and 96th Street. Built in 1926-1927, it was enlarged in 1931-1932. The sense of security depositors felt entrusting the bank with their hard-earned savings was enhanced by the imposing nature of the architecture: two major facades were dominated by giant Ionic columns that flanked the entrances on Amsterdam Avenue, and recessed double-height windows lit the main banking room on both Amsterdam Avenue and 96th Street.

Perhaps because of its majestic design, the East River Savings Bank occupied a royal position in the community—as did the Central Savings Bank at 73rd Street and Broadway—while retaining a close relationship with its customers. The bank tellers knew most of the passbook holders by name, and the passbook holders returned the favor.

If the big banks were the guardians of the big bucks, the small change could be safely deposited in an Uncle Sam's Cash Register Bank. First made in 1907 by the Durable Toy and Novelty Company, this coin bank was in use from the 1920s to the 1970s with few changes along the way.                                    rw

# Cache 22

❧

As the stock market goes up and down and our net worth follows suit, I think back lovingly on the days, in the early thirties, that my mother made her weekly deposits in her savings account at the East River Savings Bank. I liked going with her, particularly in summer, when the great hall with its marble interior and vaulted ceilings (no pun intended) provided a cool refuge from the sizzling city sidewalks.

My mother trusted the bank with her money because she knew it was not only protected by the East River Savings, but also by the newly instituted FDIC. Although she and Chicken Little had a lot in common, she had no fear of losing any portion of her principle, nor was she ever worried that the percentage of interest her money earned (compounded and stamped each time she presented her passbook) would change. I remember the interest being 3 per cent, but whatever it was, that's what it was, for as long as she had her account.

As a six- or seven-year-old, the stock market crash was not high on my list of concerns. Apparently, my father never put much stock, so to speak, in the market, so my parents didn't have any money invested when that shaky institution took its nosedive. The closest I came to experiencing the debacle was seeing my Aunt Marguerite waving some decorated parchment certificates around and bemoaning the fact they were not worth the paper they were printed on now—since The Crash.

There also was my parents' friend, Jack. Whenever his name was mentioned, everyone's eyes would roll and deep sighs, almost in unison, could be heard. It seemed that Jack, a former Wall Street stock broker who was unfortunate enough to put his money where his mouth was, had gone from "having it all" to his present "straitened" circumstances—their word, not mine. He was a tall man with very erect posture, which I naturally attributed to his "straightened" circumstances.

Although or maybe because my parents never invested in stocks or bonds or owned a home, car, or boat, my mother saved wherever she could. In addition to her East River Savings account, she owned an Uncle Sam's Cash Register Bank. Like Mama's bank account in I Remember Mama, this offered me, as a child, a great sense of security. I would watch reverently whenever she made a deposit. Sometimes I was allowed to pull down the lever as she slipped the dimes, one by one, into her bank.

This toy bank was not like any others produced in the thirties. There were no rubber stoppers to be pulled out that allowed the saver to remove the coins at will. Once you deposited the first dime, the bank was locked. It was metal: no amount of prying, thumping, or jostling could open it—I can testify to that. Every time you put a dime in the slot and pulled down the lever, the cash register rang and registered your deposit. That was it. There was no possible way of removing any of the dimes until you had $10. Then, and only then, would the little door at the bottom release and the money come spilling out. If you deposited one extra dime, even by mistake, you were out of luck—I can testify to that, too. The bank locked again and you would have to wait until it again registered $10 to open it.

I loved this bank—unconditionally; not so much for its "saving" quality as for its resemblance to a real cash register. I knew it would prove invaluable to a young "store keeper" such as myself, and it topped my birthday list the year I was nine.

My Uncle Sams's was pale blue and accepted three coins: nickels, dimes, and quarters. Unfortunately it, too, only opened at $10, not a nickel before, so making change for the customers was really not possible. In my "store," I insisted on exact change. But on the saving side, it helped establish a life-long habit of saving change, and the first time my bank opened and presented me with $10—I think it took a year—I opened my very own East River Savings Bank account. A passbook was issued in my name. (I don't remember any "in trust for" or any other qualifying words under "Lyla Blake.")

Like my mother, I seized all opportunities to save. Even before World War II, we were encouraged to participate in the Postal Saving Stamp Program at school. To join this program, children in fourth or fifth grade had to buy one 10-cent stamp a week and paste it on a card provided by the post office. All very official and very much like the foreign postage stamps I was pasting in my album at home. When I had pasted in ten 10-cent stamps, I could get a $1 savings certificate. I think I accumulated five of these in the course of my school career, and although they didn't pay for my wedding, this thought of saving a dime remains with me to this day.

The only problem is where to save it. The Postal Savings Stamps Program is long gone, and today's CDs (yesterday's savings accounts) are paying less than 1% APR (yesterday's compound interest). My mattress is so thick and heavy I'm afraid if I managed to slip my savings under it, it might come flying out each time I changed the sheets. I've considered going back to an Uncle Sam's Cash Register Bank. I saw one on eBay, vintage 1936—9 hours and 36 minutes left on the bidding—but it doesn't seem practical. Despite the market downturn, I do have a bit more money now than when I was ten, so my arm (not in such great shape) would get awfully tired pulling down that lever. And besides, with CVS now occupying the former East River Savings Bank building on 96th Street, where would I put the $10 when it opened—and opened—and opened?

# Owed to a Charge Account

O little plate,
O wondrous card,
I look at you with high regard,
Without your help, I could not own
A winter coat or telephone,
I doubt if I'd have seeds for grass
Or fifteen gallons worth of gas,
The credit you extend for dining
Enables me to eat by signing,
You're always willing to award
Me luxuries I can't afford,
And giving credit where it's due—
All things I am, I owe to you.

Good Housekeeping (March '64)

Anna Mae Wong

Sylvia Sidney

June

Merle Oberon

Olivia DeHavilland

# Putting a Good Face On It

In our house, high cheekbones were the beauty standard. My sister, June, a cosmetic expert at sixteen, had so decreed, and I, at eleven, not yet even old enough to have pimples, was hardly in a position to challenge her pronouncement.

Besides, even though it was still hard for me to find those bones on a face to start with, and then to determine how high was high enough, I saw what she meant. All the hollows in the cheeks of the most famous Hollywood stars were caused by prominent cheekbones that stood maybe half an inch below their eyes. Ann Sheridan, Rosalind Russell, Carole Lombard, Merle Oberon—all passed the cheekbone test with flying colors. Merle Oberon was June's favorite. Not only did she have the requisite bone structure, her almond-shaped eyes gave a Eurasian quality to her face that June admired and tried to replicate by extending her eyeliner up just a bit at the corner of each eye, creating just enough of an exotic effect to make people wonder if we had the same parents.

Unfortunately, June's own cheekbones were not quite as high as she would have liked. To remedy this, she applied her best makeup technique (she was already planning an acting career) and accentuated her hollows with rouge so to the casual onlooker, they looked like the real thing.

As her devoted disciple, I too longed for the kind of facial architecture I saw in the movie magazines. The problem for me was, my cheeks were anything but hollow; I only knew I had cheekbones because by pressing down hard on the area where they were supposed to be, eventually my fingers would hit pay dirt.

June tried to help me correct this deficit. When I began to wear makeup—I was a late bloomer—she lent me her rouge and showed me how to apply it, but even under her steadfast tutelage, I ended up looking like a rosy-cheeked lass from the Isle of Tralee. No way was anyone going to mistake me for Anna May Wong—another favorite of June's.

*Posing for my brother*

Luckily for me, I was not alone in my lack of depressions and distinctive facial structure. Shirley Temple and Judy Garland, my idols of the screen, had hordes of adoring fans despite their roundish rather than ovalish-shaped faces. They even allowed themselves to be photographed, cheeks and all. Maybe if I had been able to sing and dance and had corkscrew curls, I might have felt differently about my looks. But I won't lie to you, I would have given a month of penny candy to have cheekbones that were visible to the naked eye. As it was, every time I looked in the mirror and saw the slightly pudgy protuberance on either side of my face, I wondered if it was possible to lose weight just in your cheeks.

Looking back, I'm not sure whether I really bought the whole cheekbone story and wanted to look like the exotic stars June wanted to look like, or whether, in my heart of hearts, what I really wanted, whatever it entailed, was solely, simply, to look like my sister, June.

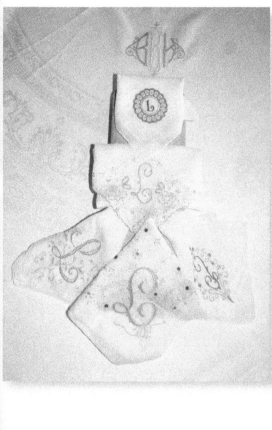

*Broadway, Schrafft's and Seeded Rye*

# Trousseau

〜✿〜

Before World War II, when I was thirteen, I found out that when a nice Jewish girl was engaged to be married, she and her mother immediately began planning her trousseau—hand-sewn nightgowns, slips, and panties; a going-away outfit; clothes for the honeymoon; and in many cases, enough of a wardrobe to carry the bride through her first year of matrimony. Her husband shouldn't have to worry.

My introduction to the process was when my sister-in-law-to-be, Jean, allowed me to sit in when she was choosing silks and laces for the lingerie that would launch her career as a wife and mother. To a thirteen-year-old—my brother was eleven years older than I—this was a scene right out of The Arabian Nights.

A gentleman, usually of foreign birth, would arrive at the house carrying large bolts of imported satins in shades of pink, ecru, and peach, and smaller rolls of handmade laces that would trim each garment, with especial attention to the peignoir and gown the bride would wear on her wedding night. This outfit might be in blue to set it apart from the other floor-length gowns made for every night use.

Although there didn't seem to be a standard list dictating how many of each—nightgowns, slips, etc.— belonged in a trousseau, everyone knew that, because a laundress usually came only once a week to wash and iron, the bride would need at least seven days' worth of lingerie to carry her through.

The seamstress whose nimble fingers and gossamer threads would transform these luxurious fabrics into luxurious garments was called "Blyman." I am not hesitant to use her real name, because given her age in the 1940s, one can only assume she is now either sewing or wearing angel wings. She was a small, retiring, unobtrusive woman, whose own clothes hung from a slight, shapeless frame. Never one to offer an opinion, unless specifically invited to do so, Blyman did weigh in on how she thought a particular satin would "make up" and, if chosen, how many yards she would need to complete the garment at hand.

There probably were many "Blymans" working in the neighborhood at that time. Ours—I say "ours" because she later made lingerie for my sister June's trousseau—seemed to have made a life catering to the needs of our extended family. The seamstress was unmarried and there was no indication she had any attachment, romantic or otherwise. The contrast between her own physical appearance and the smooth, elegant fabrics she handled was visible even to a teenager.

When Blyman had finished sewing the lingerie, some, not all, pieces were sent to be monogrammed. The initials used were the first letter of the bride's name, the first letter of the bride's maiden name, and the first letter of her married name—in Jean's case: JUB, a cause for many humorous comments. But funny or not, the order of one's initials did not deviate from the accepted form.

The hand embroidery used in monogramming was provided by the G & S Embroidery Shop at 77th Street and Broadway. There, not only lingerie, but handkerchiefs, men's shirts, sweaters, tablecloths, and napkins, all stitched in the style and color of the customer's choosing, were turned out by a few ladies in a small workroom at the back of the shop. While the store did offer machine embroidery as well at half the price, the difference was immediately apparent to the practiced eye, and all the eyes I knew were practiced, to say the least.

By the time I was married, in 1951, the Blymans of the world were few and far between, as were the exquisite silks and satins of the pre-World War II era. Gentlemen of foreign birth were no longer going house to house with bolts of imported materials because imports were in scarce supply and only a privileged few could afford to have clothes made of them for them.

The handkerchiefs for my trousseau were hand-monogrammed at G & S. The rest of my clothes—lace trimmed undies and all—were bought ready-to-wear at various department stores. But my wedding nightgown and peignoir, true to tradition, were a soft, lighter-than-sky blue.

# Plan Ahead

On the next rainy day I will go
    through the house
Like a broom at the end of a missile.
I will tear through each closet and
    straighten each drawer
And vacuum the rugs till they bristle.
I will answer those letters I've put off
    for weeks
And clean up the desk—
    not to miss one,
I will hang curtains, bake pies and
    re-laquer brass—
On the next rainy day after this one.

American Home (March '60)

# Baleboosteh—
# Mistress of the House

My mother was not the best housekeeper on the block—her friend Rose Kramer, whose cushions were perpetually fluffed, was. In Mom's terms, being the "best" meant your house was ready for "drop in" company at any hour of the day or night, although city dwellers were not likely to drop in unannounced on their friends or neighbors. A sense of formality lingered from previous times, when "receiving" hours were openly discussed and allowed receivers plenty of time to make sure all the silver had been polished (preferably with Gorham, not with one of those new dip formulas), and every last saucer had been taken out of the dish drainer.

Also in my mother's case, and that of other New Yorkers I knew, it was a point of pride not to know one's next-door neighbors. Many was the time I heard her declare to a friend—who was fortunate enough to live on the next block and was therefore eligible for friendship—"I've lived in this house for ten years and I don't know a soul." If the other woman knew a "soul" in her building, she was not about to admit it.

Blue-ribbon baleboosteh or not, my mother followed the rules of the traditional Jewish housekeeper. Although we were not orthodox, by a long shot, at Passover time she "turned over" the kitchen in her own way. To those who "keep" Kosher, "turning over" means bringing out dishes, utensils, and pots that are only used during this particular eight-day period. For us, the "turning over" meant coming home from school one day, usually in April, and finding my mother and a helper taking all the dishes, pots, and pans out of the cabinets; washing out the cabinets, which were lined corner to corner with oilcloth; scrubbing everything; drying everything; and putting each dish or pot back in its former place. Even if a family did not observe the dietary laws, the concept of cleanliness in relation to anything that had to do with food trickled down, and our kitchen was no exception. After a dinner party, the kitchen floor was not only swept, it was washed before my mother went to bed. She might not have done the washing herself, but someone made sure no harm would come to anyone who chose to eat off our linoleum floor.

While the kitchen "turnover" was not a big turn-on for me as a child--I doubt if I would even have noticed anything out of the ordinary when I came home from school during the big cleanup, if I hadn't found it hard to dig out a glass for my milk or the box of Oreo cookies— what I did notice, and loved, was "change over" time for the rest of the house. This took place soon after Decoration Day (or Memorial Day, as it is now known). Summer was coming, and in preparation for the hot months ahead, all the upholstered furniture in the living and dining rooms—the couch, the chairs, the loveseats—was fitted out with made-to-order cotton slipcovers, whose light and airy flowers, stripes, and plaids seemed immediately to cool off each room.

The carpets were rolled up and sent out to be cleaned, leaving the floors bare, the perfect surface for a budding tap dancer—even Fred Astaire was never asked to dance on an oriental rug. But the best time of all was just after Labor Day, at summer's end, when the rugs, rolled in brown paper, were returned to our house. The rooms in most of the old apartment buildings were large (even the width was at least fifteen feet), so there was plenty of room for three or four of us to climb on top of the long roll and jump off—climb on top and jump off— climb on top and jump off. What a game. Of course it only lasted a few days, until the rugs were unwrapped and put down, and it only happened once a year, but the excitement of it ran a close second to the start of the marble season.

At about the time my mother was "summerizing" our home, the building management, at 104th Street and Broadway, was doing its share to see that the tenants were kept as comfortable as possible during the summer months. In late spring, handymen attached black and white striped canvas awnings to every window in the apartment, shutting out the glaring rays of the sun and, unfortunately, a good deal of the summer light.

The city, too, did its part in cooling off the neighborhood. Huge water trucks would suddenly appear to spray the sizzling sidewalks and create at least a temporary respite from the summer heat.

Over my mother's strong objections, my father had an air conditioner installed in their bedroom window when we moved to 82nd Street in 1939. It was turned on only occasionally because of my mother's strongly held belief that going from a cold room into a warm one or vice versa lowered one's resistance and hence could lead to pneumonia, with possibly a stopover at a head cold.

Since all proper housekeeping was done by the housewife to keep the family healthy and comfortable, my mother's opposition to mechanical help may simply have been, she didn't feel quite safe with anything she couldn't wash, dry, and put away herself.

I remember Levy's. Do you remember Morris Brothers, where we went to order labels with our name on them to sew into the backs of our clothes if we were going to camp? (Amanda Nash)

I'm an old timer, born at 55 W. 83rd. St. in 40's. I grew up with Florence Bakery on Bdway. After attending Sunday 9:00 mass at HTC, the treat for the week was a visit to Florence's for their famous "Charlotte Russe", such a wonderful memory (Harriet Spina)

Charlotte Russe was my brothers favorite (lee nickelsburg). I loved the 7 layer cake the best. I grew up at 221 W 82nd and had the very best childhood. Who remembers the boat ride outside of rappaports (next to Levy Bros)? (Linda Weiss)

We used to buy 1/2 a cake at Cake Masters for our daughter's half birthday (Margaret Ryan)

These are wonderful memories! I have not thought about Cake Master's or Levy's Stationary Store for many years! (Johanna Damgaard Liander)

I remember Rappaports. My mom would take me there for shoes, they put your feet in a thermography machine to make sure the fit was right... Who remembers Kitty Kelly & A.S. Beck shoes on Broadway next to Schraffts...? (Harriet Spina)

# I Can Get It for You Retail

Broadway in our neighborhood was retail heaven. There were grocery stores; bakeries; haberdasheries; lingerie shops; shoe stores for men, women, and children; fish markets; stationery stores; shoe repair shops; candy stores; drug stores; milliners; and then ten blocks further on there were grocery stores, haberdasheries, lingerie shops, shoe stores . . . . Each mini-neighborhood had its own retail support system, and each family knew which store was "the best." Fortunately for the store owners, opinions differed: my mother thought the lox was less salty at the little appetizer store on the west side of Broadway; Selma's mother thought the lox was less salty at the little appetizer store on 91st Street—so both stores stayed in business. Although neither of us had even tasted smoked salmon at that time, I knew my mother was right and Selma knew her mother was right, a point we vehemently proclaimed between rounds of jump rope.

Although my mother's rating system covered quality stores in most categories—she bought my father's white-on-white shirts only from Briggs's on Broadway and 85th Street, and my father bought her alligator bags only from The Plymouth Shop on Broadway and 82nd Street—when it came to products that might affect my brother's, sister's, or my physical well- being, the "best" took on a new meaning. Shoes to support the malleable bones in our feet were such an item. In her view (and what other views were there?) Indian Walk was the only shoe store fit to fit our feet.

I can't say I remember when I traded my booties in for my first real shoes—high white lace-ups—but I was told these and all others of descending height were bought at our local Indian Walk Shoe Store. Before school opened in the fall (always after Labor Day), and in the spring, before Easter, I could look forward to getting new shoes. Possibly because I knew the ritual would end with an Indian Walk balloon tied to my wrist, I participated willingly in the process.

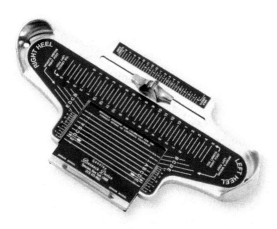

First, at the salesman's request, I would stand up and place my foot on a metal device, heel against the back, while a clerk, specially trained in fitting children's shoes, pushed a slider toward my big toe, stopping just short of the mark. The grooved ruler on either side indicated the length and width of the shoe you would need, usually at least one size up from the one you were wearing. Until I was nine or ten, for school days I had my choice of brown oxfords with brown shoelaces or brown oxfords with brown shoelaces—nothing less would do to hold my bones together. If I was so bold as to suggest I might possibly like a different style, my mother described in graphic detail what could happen to a child's foot if left unsupported: had I seen any ducks recently?

Noticed their splayed feet? How would I feel if my un-supported lasts were spread across the floor? I wasn't sure what "splayed" meant, but I got the picture, and it wasn't until saddle shoes came into style, and Indian Walk and my mother declared them safe, that I got any relief from the drab brown everyday shoes. I did, how-ever, get to have shiny black patent leather Mary Jane's for weekends and holidays, and sneakers for camp until it became clear I was never going to be a tennis player.

If our feet were a major concern, imagine where our stomachs stood. Food, undisputedly vital for our health and well-being, had to be of the finest quality. That's where Citarella came in. At that time only a neighborhood fish market, it stood at first place in the Betty Blake consumer report. I don't think Mom had spoken to any fishermen personally, but she was con-vinced Citrarella's fish was rushed from hook to store without passing "Go." According to her, you could "taste the freshness." I would have been happy to take her word for it and skip the fish. When we asked "What's for dinner?" and the answer was "Fish," a gen-eral groan went up. Nevertheless, once a week there it was on the plate where the steak should have been. Our complaints went unheeded—fish, after all, was brain food; the only concession my mother made was to try and make the unwanted meal more palatable. One of her favorite ways of disguising the ingredient was the Halibut Ring from her cooking Bible, The Settlement Cook Book, another "best" in her book. The Joy of Cooking could not be mentioned in the same breath.

## Halibut Ring

| | |
|---|---|
| 2 lbs. halibut . . . . . . . . . . . . . | 4 eggs, separated |
| 3 tablespoons butter . . . . . . . . | 1 pint cream whipped |
| 2 tablespoons flour . . . . . . . . . | 1 lb. fresh shrimp |
| 1/2 cup cream or milk . . . . . . . | Hollandaise Sauce |
| 1 teaspoon salt . . . . . . . . . . . | 1 tablespoon |
| | chopped pimentos |

*Boil halibut, following recipe for Boiled Fish, page 131. Remove skin and bone. Grind flesh very fine. Heat butter, add flour when it bubbles, add 1/2 cup cream, stir until smooth, add salt, and stir gradually into the well-beaten yolks. Stir in the minced fish and when cool, add stiffly beaten whites of eggs, and lastly fold in the whipped cream. Put in a well-greased ring mold, dotted with bits of pimento, place in a moderate oven in a pan of boiling water, and bake about ¾ hour or until well set. Remove to serving platter and in center place hot Boiled Shrimp, page 149.*

The eggs, the cream, and the butter were all so delectable, we couldn't help thinking how great the dish would be if only it didn't have the fish.

Though all food was not as vital to our health, the rye bread from Cake Masters was incomparable, as was tub butter from Daitch's (where else was it creamery fresh?) and sturgeon from Barney Greengrass (in a class by itself). These choices proved my mother's dedication to quality and knowing where to shop. And we had no reason to doubt her authority: when it came to food, clothes, or home goods in our family, it was generally agreed—Mother knew "bests." Oh, and by the way: Was that fish thing fact or fiction? Hard to prove—it might just be coincidence that we all turned out to be so brilliant.

# Buy Now—Flee Later

From all I've read and heard it said it
Seems I'm good for endless credit;
Every bank is frantically
Trying to give loans to me,
Buy a house, a car, a yacht,
No one cares what cash I've got,
Take a European vacation,
Money waits in any nation,
No one seems a bit concerned
Lending me more than I've earned,
Clearly in the marketplace,
I'm a credit to my race.

Wall Street Journal (June '66)

*245 West 104th Street*

*375 Riverside Drive*

*470 West End Avenue*

*Broadway, Schrafft's and Seeded Rye*

# High (Rise) Living

❧

My brother, George, always described life in an apartment house as living on a shelf. In the first apartment I remember, on 104th Street, our "shelf" was on the fourth floor, where we occupied a roomy three-bedroom, two bath plus maid's room and bath in a sixteen-story building.

I didn't know, at the time, that I lived in a "high rise" building—that term is relatively new, not more than thirty or forty years old. To me it was just tall and had an elevator. Although West End Avenue seemed to have mostly "tall" buildings, there were still a few "shorter" houses, fewer than six stories high, in between the big ones. According to law, these had to have fire escapes.

In and around Amsterdam and Columbus Avenues, there were many brownstones, formerly single-family homes, now divided into small apartments that provided shelter for multiple families, many of them immigrants. In summer, people who lived in these crowded apartments would open up the fire hydrants, and cool water would cascade down the street, providing some relief from the stifling heat. This was illegal, and probably still is. If a policeman was around, the offending party, assuming he could be found, was given a summons or just a strong reprimand. But when the temperature reached 90 or 95 degrees, there were not enough police in the entire city to prevent the march of crime.

Most of my friends lived in buildings similar to mine—a few in what would now be called "midrise"— maybe twelve-story elevator buildings with slightly smaller apartments. I only learned about one-family homes, surrounded by grass and trees, from the moving pictures, where I marveled at children as young as I was, able to ride their bicycles on quiet roads, unaccompanied, even by an older sister.

In my world, going to play outside involved taking the elevator to the street floor—dragging my doll carriage down four flights of stairs was not practical— and meeting other "little mothers." We would walk our "babies" up and down the sidewalk, and when we tired of motherhood, we might go on to another game, which was all right as long as we didn't stray too far from the front door of the apartment building where, it was understood, the doorman was keeping an unofficial eye on us.

A big advantage to living in an apartment building that had almost ninety apartments was the number of children a child of almost any age could find to play with. My friend Mickey lived a few stories over me: we could run up and down stairs without involving the elevator man. Weekend nights was when apartment living really paid off. At eight or nine years old we would not have been allowed to go out in the dark; living in the same house, we could get together in one or the other of our apartments and play to our hearts' content— sometimes sleeping over without needing anyone to walk us home.

The inside stairs also provided an opportunity for games—seeing how many steps we could jump from and still land on our feet. There were a few risks to this game, which made it all the more exciting. A sprained ankle or visible bruise might alert a parent to how we had been entertaining ourselves, and for a while the stairs would be off limits, even for inter-apartment visiting. When things quieted down, we would resume our game. I think my topper was six steps with both my ankles intact.

As I we got a little older and were allowed to walk around the corner or cross a side street to play with a friend, we began to choose which houses were more child-friendly. Our elevator man, Lenny, got a bit testy if we wanted to go up and down too often, but Suzy's elevator man was downright mean—one trip up and one trip down, no exceptions. This meant Suzy came to my house more often than I went to hers. Some houses had rules against playing handball against the building or even drawing a hopscotch on the sidewalk in front of the building—although, as we were quick to point out, they didn't own the sidewalk. Sadly, I had not entered my Letters to the Editor period, or you can bet the whole city would have been aware of this grave miscarriage of justice.

Considering all the opportunity they provided for play, and the protective environment afforded their residents, apartment buildings were not the cool, impersonal monoliths their stone and cement exterior suggested. Awnings stretched from the top of the front entrance to the curb, shielding anyone going in or out of the house from rain or snow; doormen very often walked the dogs of owners who could not make it outside that day and were the repository of messages or deliverer of special packages, knowing each family member, even the smallest child, by name.

If home is where the heart is, shelf or no shelf, I always knew where I lived.

# Broadway

After the Civil War, a commission including Theodore Roosevelt senior (the father of the president) and the infamous William "Boss" Tweed changed the street map of Manhattan to widen Bloomingdale Road from 59th Street north to 106th Street. It included plans for a thirty-foot-wide strip of cultivated parkland in the middle, plus the planting of elm trees on both sides of this avenue, which was then renamed The Boulevard. This plan was obviously inspired by the work of Baron Hausmann in creating the network of boulevards like the Champs-Élysées in Paris.

Unfortunately for the elm trees, the demand for development of residences and transportation, particularly north of 72nd Street, spurred the building of the IRT subway from 59th Street north. The company used the cut-and-cover method of tunneling from 1904 to 1907. When completed, the only vestige of the original plan was the unpaved center strip. The name of this wide avenue was changed to Broadway in 1899, and upon completion of the subway construction, the center strip was landscaped to include trees, shrubs, flowers, and two oversize park benches at each end of each section, or nearly two hundred benches.

No other North/South Avenue, including the landscaped Park Avenue, offered this benefit for local residents. rw

# The Middle

The Upper West Side in the 1930s and early 1940s did-
n't lack for park benches where mothers could sit with
other mothers and chat while their children played on
grassy areas Robert Moses had provided in his Grand
Plan for Riverside Drive Park. For those families who
lived closer to Central Park, plenty of benches stood in
country-like areas, and afternoons saw residents resting
on similar benches, visiting with neighbors and friends.

Many older people, mostly women, did not
choose to walk the two or three blocks east or west of
Broadway to a park. Instead, they left their homes in the
morning or after lunch and headed for The Middle, a
grassy strip of land, fenced on the sides and paved at
each end, that separated uptown from downtown traffic
on Broadway; the streetcar tracks stood on either side of

it. And at each crossing, from 72nd Street to a least 115th Street, there were two wide benches where elderly residents sat and passed the time talking to each other about their children, their grandchildren, and "the old country." Although the "old country" was not the same for all of them, they were able to communicate using a language common to all—Yiddish.

*Before the Middle 1906*

My grandmother was one of these ladies. Having come to America from Hungary as a young bride, she and her husband (my grandfather) settled in St. Louis, Missouri, where, despite the fact Grandpa was an itinerant cantor, they had nine children over the course of fifteen years. Widowed at a young age, Grandma Regina moved the family to New York City. The oldest daughter, Marguerite, in her early twenties, became the chief breadwinner. Working in retailing, she soon was promoted to buyer of women's dresses and eventually owner of a retail store on Madison Avenue. As the brothers and sisters moved away, Marguerite, who remained single, made a home for her mother and herself on the Upper West Side, not far from where our family lived. It was there my grandmother joined her friends, bundled up against the cold or protected from the heat, to reminisce or commiserate about what was going on in their lives.

Nobody is quite sure who actually planned "The Middle," but for these women and many who came after them, these oases were truly a "mitzvah."

*Broadway, Schrafft's and Seeded Rye*

# My Brother, the Genius

Anyone who knows anything about Jewish families knows where the son is in the pecking order—particularly if he is the eldest with two younger sisters. And if he happens to be a genius. . .well, you can just imagine.

Luckily for us, my brother, George, despite his reported 185 I.Q., was also a kind, witty, personable fellow who was a lot more than the sum of his talents, which everyone, even those outside the family, knew were considerable.

Because he was almost eleven years older than I, the details of his early childhood were not known to me. My memories begin when I was about six and he was sixteen, still living at home in our three-bedroom apartment on 104th Street. My sister and I shared the second bedroom. His, as I recall, was larger than ours, probably because it had to encompass all the paraphernalia he needed to pursue his ever-growing interests. These ran from music to photography to writing to electric trains.

I don't know if he was ever offered piano lessons when he was a child. I was led to believe he was self-taught, and I do remember when he began playing, or more accurately, banging out "The Continental." By that time I was taking piano lessons from an experienced teacher who played each piece before assigning it to me, so I knew what good playing sounded like, and George's wasn't it. But I also knew that he couldn't read music. He had sounded out "The Continental" by ear, playing with two hands and improvising chords, and wasn't my brother amazing? In later life, his "ear" led him to a successful collaboration with Dick Liebert, a composer and organist at Radio City Music Hall. George wrote the lyrics to Liebert's music and became a member of ASCAP. The royalties he earned from one song alone, "Come Dance With Me," paid the college tuitions for his three children.

Going back to his passions as a teenager: at the same time he was loving music, learning to play piano, and balancing popular music with classical, he discovered the art of photography and was carried away with

its creative possibilities. This newfound interest didn't go unnoticed by our parents. Almost immediately after announcing his intention to become a photographer, he was given first a Graflex, a popular camera used mostly by professionals—no Brownie box cameras for him— and later a Leica, manufactured in pre-World War II Germany.

As was his wont, he learned everything he could about using the tools of his new trade, and then, with a high school friend acting as his assistant, set up a business taking pictures at children's parties, sons and daughters feted by their well-to-do families in their luxurious homes on the Upper East Side. He was able to develop these negatives and make prints without leaving our apartment: my mother had seen to that. As soon as it became apparent that this seventeen-year-old was exhibiting yet another talent, he was given "the maid's room," a small room found in two- or three-bedroom apartments in the 30s and 40s to be used by sleep-in help. Since no one was living with us at the time, George was able to convert this space into a darkroom, with all the developing equipment needed to produce quality black-and-white prints for his growing list of customers.

Being his father's son, of course, it wasn't long before still photography fell second to his new love—moving pictures. With the money earned from his party work, George was able to purchase a 16mm movie camera. Now he was in the home-movies business, and darned if he wasn't good at that, too.

Unlike many of my friends' older brothers, my brother never objected to having me hang around when his friends came over to listen to Benny Goodman records or play poker. In fact, they often let me sit in. Even at eight years old, I knew my flushes from my straights, and because I supplied the refreshments— butter spritz cookies were my specialty—I received many proposals of marriage from the appreciative players, who also supplied me with the pennies I used to ante up.

It would be wrong to leave the impression that my sister June and I were shortchanged because we stood on lower rungs of the family ladder. We weren't. We were supported and indulged almost as much as George was. Almost, but not quite, He was, after all, The Son.

# Fountain Lunch

Madam, please remove your pallid
Features from my chicken salad.
It is understood this highchair
Will be your chair after my chair.
But I cannot see that beating
On my neck will spur my eating,
And despite your ho and humming,
I have shadow layer cake coming.
May I say statistics show where
Battery will get you nowhere,
Yesterday, need I remind you,
You ate lunch with me behind you

Collier's (September '51)

# Our Restaurants

In 1898, Frank Shattuck bought out his major candy supplier, William J. Schrafft, and began to expand his business by turning his chain of candy stores into tearoom/restaurants where the ladies who lunch could lunch. Setting ego aside, he called the restaurants "Schrafft's," and by 1915 had nine stores in Manhattan, one in Brooklyn, one in Syracuse, and the Boston headquarters. By 1923, the number had grown to twenty-two stores; by 1934, thirty-four; and by 1968, the company boasted a grand total of fifty-five Schrafft's.

Small or large, the front of each store was devoted to a tantalizing array of candy—chocolates that could be bought in boxes of all shapes and sizes—and other sugary goodies displayed in immaculate glass-fronted cases.

In our Schrafft's, and in most, the candy section was opposite the soda fountain, where customers could sit at the counter and order lighter fare, sandwiches, and ice cream concoctions. In the dining room beyond, young women, invariably newly arrived Irish, wearing white aprons over black uniforms, hair neatly tucked into fine mesh hairnets, waited table. Little known were Schrafft's policies concerning women. The company was among the first to hire women as managers and had a profit-sharing program as well as a pregnancy program for expectant employees.

The Tip Toe Inn at the corner of Broadway and 86th Street was a Jewish delicatessen founded by Aaron Chinitz in 1918. From the beginning, the Tip Toe was a gathering place where friends could meet and eat what was described as "haute Jewish cuisine": cheesecake, lox, gefilte fish, and borscht. The store opened up into a large, airy dining room with thick white tablecloths and formally attired waiters who presented the menu that usually included not-too-lean corned beef and peppery pastrami. Cholesterol had not yet been discovered.

Because Steinberg's, at 84th and Broadway, was a kosher dairy restaurant, it also appealed to vegetarians. (Fish was considered kosher; meat was not.) The menu included blintzes, cheese products, vegetarian stuffed cabbage, and a host of other meatless, Eastern-European-style dishes.

rw

# My Love Affair
# with Schrafft's

For many transported New Yorkers, the memory of corned beef or hot pastrami sandwiches on Jewish rye lingers years after they've moved to less ethnically oriented locations. I, on the other hand, eschewing the food of my people, think longingly of a chopped egg (celery never added) sandwich on toasted cheese bread (crusts removed); a hot butterscotch sundae; vanilla ice cream, topped with just a soupcon of whole salted almonds; or that paragon of fizzy drinks: a Broadway soda, chocolate with coffee ice cream.

This Waspy fare that set my taste buds aflutter was served at a restaurant called Schrafft's at 82nd Street and Broadway, around the corner from where lived. There were more than thirty Schrafft's located throughout the City. The menu was the same in all and only varied slightly from day to day: Monday might be creamed chicken on toast; Tuesday, pan-browned lamb hash. They offered the comfort food of the day: well-prepared, simple, and totally American cuisine.

In the early years, the Schrafft's closest to my home was closest to my heart. That's where my love affair with this purveyor of all things sweet began. In the high school years, things got serious. Hunter College

High School, where I began my secondary school experience, was located between 67th and 68th Streets on Lexington Avenue. During the war years (need I specify World War II?), the army used our building in the afternoons for training purposes.

To accommodate their needs, our school day began at 8 A.M. and ended at 1 P.M. We were on our own for lunch.

Happily for us, there was a small, counter-only Schrafft's at the corner of 68th Street and Madison Avenue where, for less than a dollar, we could have a crustless sandwich (35 cents) and ice cream (20 cents) served in a small metal pedestal dish just large enough to hold the single well-trimmed scoop carefully meted out by Eric, our friendly counterman. Schrafft's was known for its dainty, precise portions—all servers were trained not to leave any jagged edges that might provide an extra spoonful for the customer. Although we were well aware of the odds against us, each day we watched intently, hoping against hope this would be the day Eric's hand would slip and we would end up with just a little more of our cherished dessert. It never happened.

By the time I emerged from my teens, Schrafft's and I were going steady. Aside from an occasional Chock Full O' Nuts dated-nut cream cheese sandwich, lunch out meant eating at Schrafft's. Because they were scattered throughout the city, the restaurants were not hard to find. If we were shopping midtown, we ate at the one on Madison and 58th Street. If we were further uptown on the East Side we ate at the one on East 79th Street. My husband, then boyfriend, worked downtown and, because he was so secure and didn't mind being the only male customer on the premises, we would often meet at the Schrafft's on 13th Street and Fifth Avenue near his office. Unlike the others that had strictly vintage tearoom décor, this building, with its rounded exterior and chrome interior, was pretty "modern." The food was the same, but the bar in this particular location was quite active. Here, Manhattans and Old Fashioneds were almost as popular as the ice cream sodas.

In the summer of 1949, when I was a guest editor at Mademoiselle Magazine, and engaged in a whirlwind of arranged activities, I was so happy to slip away occasionally for lunch at Schrafft's a block away from the Chanin Building, on East 42nd Street, where I was working. A little chubby from my college days, I eschewed the delights of my youth and instead, every day, ate a hot vegetable plate accompanied by a glass of buttermilk. I might have lost weight even if I had opted for a less wholesome main dish. Schrafft's serving portions would have done today's Weight Watchers proud. How many points are there in one loin lamb chop?

Schrafft's held my heart until the last recognizable restaurant closed in the 1970s. Although the ice cream continued to be sold in supermarkets and some ice cream stores, just seeing the familiar logo didn't do it for me. This creamy confection was not meant to be piled two or three scoops high, dripping at the edges, on a sugar cone. It was meant to be served in its little metal dish, one clean scoop—just the way Eric served it.

# My Spare Lady

A woman may cut calories
At any given time if she's
Just chanced to step
   on someone's scale
And found that she's no longer frail,
Or if she happened to espy
Her own rear view as she walked by.
A husband's quip could
   start her thinking,
How many sodas she's been drinking,
All these, admittedly, add stresses,
But nothing hurts like
   last year's dresses.

Good Housekeeping (May '63)

**Milk and Egg League Does Its Share**

Turning the first shovelful of earth for their new unit at Duarte, leaders of the Milk and Egg League, New York, are shown left to right: Mrs. Mollie Facter, Mrs. M. L. Cramer, Mrs. Ben K. Blake, Mrs. Rosenblatt, Mrs. Harry L. Charnes, Mrs. Marian Cohen, Mrs. Harry Gans, and President Mark Carter of the City of Hope.

# My Mother, the Dieter

The first time I heard the word "diet" I was nine years old, and my mother was visiting me at camp. "Well," she said, after we had exchanged our initial hugs and kisses, "do you notice anything different about me?" She was wearing a turban I didn't think I had seen before. No, that wasn't it. Her eyes were still blue—her shoes? Wrong again. Without waiting for any more guesses, she outlined her waist with her hands. "I've lost twenty pounds—I've been on a diet!"

That my mother thought she was too fat was not news to me. As long as I could remember, she talked about how beautiful her figure was before she had children. (Had my birth caused that girth?) She also bemoaned her love of bread, rice, and spaghetti—starches she shunned as villains in her war against weight. But at nine I was still skinny and didn't particularly like bread, rice, or spaghetti, so I didn't pay much attention to weight, hers or mine. Still, she was obviously so pleased with her new look, I listened patiently as she described the Metropolitan Life Diet that had, in her words, changed her life. It was all very easy—small portions, three meals a day, no eating in between. A little pamphlet, issued by the insurance company, showed menus of suggested meals for a week, all foods carefully selected from the five major food groups. "A diet for life," Mom declared. "I can live on this forever."

And it did seem like forever to me, because while my mother was on this diet, she stopped baking—too much of a temptation—and the emphasis on healthy foods, as opposed to mayonnaise sandwiches on white bread, my favorite, was pretty hard to take. In real time, her resolution only lasted for three or four months, but by the time I had learned to bake my own cookies, her portions had grown a little larger than the Metropolitan had in mind and the pounds began to return.

I don't know what the scale had to show before my mother decided it was again time to "lose a few pounds." Then out came the little booklet, and our meals took on an overly Metropolitan Life quality. I only know not too many months after each lapse, the weight game started again. Although that particular diet faded into history, Mom had learned how to lose weight and so she did—over and over again. I don't remember a time when she wasn't on a diet or wasn't absolutely sure that this time she was losing the weight for good. She was so sure, she would have all her clothes taken in, only to return to the dressmaker, embarrassed to admit she was no longer able to zip up her skirt. She was so self-conscious about her size, she never allowed herself to be photographed straight on. In a group she was always in the second row, with only her face showing, or if alone she stood behind a table, or held something large in front of her so she appeared, or thought she did, much slimmer than she actually was.

Several times a year, she and her friends decided they needed a little prompting to shed pounds and headed for the nearest "milk farm," where they lived on a diet of milk and vegetables, usually for at least a week. For my mother and her pals, it was Marble Hall in Rye, New York. Located on the Long Island Sound, Marble Hall was a beautiful estate formerly owned by Albert

Warner, one of the five Warner brothers who founded the film studio. Rose Warner Charnas, a sister of the Warner boys—there were eleven children in all—belonged to the same organization as my mother, the Milk (no connection to the farm) and Egg League, a charity that raised money for a tubercular sanitarium in California.

While at the farm, the ladies didn't just drink milk, they exercised. Dressed in casual skirts, sweaters, and oxford shoes bought for the occasion, they took long walks around the premises and occasionally into town, where it was not unheard of for one or more of the dieters to fill in the gaps with a small bag of cookies, purchased en route and polished off before returning to the farm.

When Mom came home from Marble Hall, we all knew what to expect. Fired up from her loss of four or five pounds in a week, she would vow to stay on the milk diet and just add a few healthful foods: maybe a steak (protein); and a baked potato (potassium) with just a dab of butter to moisten the dry interior. But as the portions increased in size, so did Mom, and once again the dressmaker sprang into action. It didn't take her long to expand the waistline; she just had to put back the extra material she'd saved from the month before.

# The Wonder Years

❧

I have always been a fiercely loyal person, as was my mother before me. No private labels or generics for us: Bayer was aspirin; Kleenex was tissues; and Bumble Bee was the only canned salmon it was safe to eat.

In our house there was Hellman's Mayonnaise and Heinz Ketchup; Gulden's Mustard and Hershey's Syrup; Del Monte Asparagus and Hebrew National Salami; Oreo Cookies and Ritz Crackers. Even as a child I knew the Sunshine Biscuit Company, with its Oreo wannabe, Hydrox, was not in the same league as Nabisco, whose Social Teas, Mallomars, and Fig Newtons stood proudly on our pantry shelves, as did Kellogg's Corn Flakes, the only real corn flakes. Post's was an imposter, my mother said so. How then, I wondered, had the cereal company's founder, Marjorie Merriweather Post, grown so rich without anyone in our family buying her cereal?

Before World War II, shops specializing in cheese were un-American. Let me rephrase that. Cheese shops did not exist in America. You wanted brie? You went to a French restaurant. There were dairy stores in New York City—Daitch was one where we bought tub butter, a pound of incredibly creamy, recently churned butter a clerk scooped out of a large wooden tub. Cheese was cut to order from a solid brick of American or Cheddar bought from an American dairy. But mostly we, and other families we knew, got our pasteurized, packaged cheeses from Kraft—only. Although we drank

Borden's milk, their cream cheese never made it to our table. Our cream cheese had to be Philadelphia, a Kraft label, and a "glass" of Roka Spread was always on hand to stuff the celery stalks or smear on our Ritz crackers. Once emptied, the little glasses with their cheery painted flowers were pressed—correction, ushered—into service as juice glasses. Velveeta, another Kraft label, was my mother's choice to top her family-famous apple pie. In 2002, this smooth, American-like "cheese" was dealt a blow by the FDA when that agency notified Kraft that Velveeta could not be sold as a "cheese;" it had to be labeled a cheese product because it contained less than 51% cheese. My mother would never have gone along with that ruling (or the repudiation of her choice).

I think I had been married for twenty years before I bought Chicken of the Sea instead of Bumble Bee; or entertained the wild notion that maybe, just maybe, my cotton balls didn't have to be Johnson & Johnson; or my marshmallows Campfire. The first time I used Breck Shampoo instead of Conti's Castile, I thought my hair would fall out on the spot.

For anyone out there who's thinking this relic is really inflexible, wait just a minute. Years ago I began mixing Keeblers with my Nabisco and Carolina with my Uncle Ben's. But Social Teas are still the "crust" for my lemon chiffon pie because there is just no substitute for them. And hard as it is to find, Softasilk remains my flour of choice for a layer cake. Yeah, yeah, I know, you can adjust the measurements and use enriched—but whose birthday cake am I going to try it on?

Time marches on, and I've had to make some adjustments. My husband came to me eating King Oscar sardines; we always had Granadaisa. Of course I bought him what he was used to, but after a number of years in which I kept a stock of both brands, I put a few of the tiny brislings on my plate by mistake one day, and to my surprise found they were quite edible. Result? My children grew up never even knowing their mother had made a major compromise early in her marriage.

Russ's family also liked Green Giant Peas and Fanning's Bread and Butter Pickles, two products I was totally unfamiliar with. I don't know if anyone else makes bread and butter pickles, but I don't plan to find out.

I'm always grateful my father never had to live in a world without Hoffman's Pale Dry Ginger Ale. How could he have made the switch to Canada Dry after all the years he turned it down every time it was offered?

Despite their strict upbringing, I never tried to influence my children's preferences. I just thought if they were only served Breakstone's butter, they would, in turn, only serve Breakstone's butter. I was wrong. It actually makes me quite sad to see some of the choices they, as adults, have made. Gulden giving way to Grey Poupon was not so bad, and Pepperidge Farm Cookies can be a fairly decent substitute for Nabisco. But at a recent Passover dinner, my daughter served Streit's Matzohs instead of the Manischevitz she grew up with, and when questioned did not have the grace to lie and say the A&P had run out of Manischevitz. Instead, she announced defiantly: "My family likes Streit's."

At first I was despondent; then my glass-is-half-full nature took over, and I found it a comfort to know that, while she may not have stayed with the brand our family had used for generations, she did choose a brand, albeit a lesser one. And I realized I should be grateful for small favors. She could have bought one of those generic Israeli matzohs no one's ever heard of. Streit's? I can live with that—until it's my turn to do Passover.

*Dad on location in Bermuda*

*Broadway, Schrafft's and Seeded Rye*

# My Father the Director

სოუ

Neither my mother nor my father thought going to school every day was a big deal, particularly for a fourth grader, so every so often, on a weekday during the racing season, I would go to the track with my Dad. Usually that meant Aqueduct, in Queens, only a taxi ride away, and of course I jumped at the chance.

Although my father was not a great conversationalist—he could have been the inspiration for the 1950s movie, The Quiet Man—he seemed to enjoy having me with him. We didn't exchange confidences. I didn't tell him about the boy in school who dipped my braids in the inkwell, and he didn't tell me about the client who got away. Mostly we shared a Racing Form, and after reading about this horse or that's past performances, the odds, and the handicapping records, I would place the $2 he had given me on the horse with the prettiest name. After all, it was a horse race, even a Babbling Brook had as much chance as Seabiscuit. If my horse won I got to keep my winnings, but even if my horse lost, it was a win-win deal for me. Dad would cover my losses and enable me to stay in the race—so to speak.

Because my sister and brother, in high school and college, respectively, at the time, could not go along on these excursions, my father made sure they did not suffer financially. Each time he came home from the races he shared his winnings with the three of us. I was too young at the time to question how he always seemed to win, and if George or June had any suspicions, they didn't share them with me---or him.

That's not to say, Dad was a big time gambler who left his wife sobbing and wringing her hands while he bet the rent money on a horse—I never saw him bet more than $5, and he only went to the races when he was in between productions. But it was when he was in production, the fun began for me. On the days he was shooting I would race over to Reeves Sound Studio on West 57th Street as soon as my half day at Hunter was over, and pick my way through the wires and cameras and lights to watch the "silent" Ben Blake, give crisp directions to the actors and crew until each scene was just the way he wanted it. His gesture to informality was wearing a sweater vest instead of a matching worsted under the jacket of his dark suit. Otherwise, in his pin-striped suit, white on white shirt, tie and soft grey Fedora he might have been any businessman sitting in the canvas Director's chair. From this vantage point, he engaged in easy banter and seemed to be well-liked by everyone who worked with him; so well liked that this man, who, it was intimated, never went to high school, was one of the most successful producer/directors of short subjects in the country in the 1930's and 1940's.

One of the highlights of these afternoons spent on the set was meeting the "star" of whatever short subject they were shooting. It didn't make any difference whether I had ever heard of Henny Youngman, Penny Singleton, Allen Jenkins—at the time, they seemed like celebrities---I was dazzled by the almost Hollywood-glamour in the atmosphere and loved watching the mechanics of the production.

Before each scene, a member of the crew would hold up a slate with the scene information written on it in chalk, and two hinged sticks on top. When they were ready to shoot, the crewman would raise the slate, announce loudly, Scene 3 take 2, and then "Sticks" as he clapped the two hinged sticks together in front of the camera. As if that was not proof enough I was watching a real movie in progress, between "takes," the makeup man would rush on stage to dab at the actor's face with a large powder puff to dry up any offending spot of perspiration that might have popped up on a chin, a forehead, a cheek after the poor Thespian had spent more than an hour under the cruel glare of the omnipresent Klieg lights.

The sets were usually routine affairs: a living room; a small café; a stage—except for two that carried over into our home. Fitting perfectly into a corner of our large foyer at 470 was a walk-in bar that had been custom made to grace the grand living room of some make-believe mogul. When the week of shooting was over, it seemed a shame just to discard this handsome pickled pine entity, so Dad had it moved to our apartment, complete with bar stools, and many was the party he bartended standing behind the counter dispensing drinks. I think he preferred mixing drinks to mixing with the guests.

The second set was the interior of a grocery store, shelves stocked with cans of tuna fish (Bumble Bee) and sardines,(Granadasia) boxes of Cornflakes (Kellogg's) and cookies( Nabisco, of course.) After the shoot, the goodies were shared by all, but we ended up with enough boxes of Oreos and Mallomars to make me queen of the neighborhood for the next 6 months..

Not all of Dad's shorts were filmed in a studio; some were shot on location—Miami—a fashion show on the grounds of the elegant Roney Plaza Hotel where peacocks walked freely among the guests; Bermuda—at a time when horse-driven carriages and bicycles were the only vehicles permitted on "Pleasure Island;" the milk farms of Borden's Dairies where the process of milk production, cow to bottle, was filmed and later shown in neighborhood schools, mine included.

What always amazed me was how empty the house felt when my quiet Dad was away. His contribu-

tion to our dinner conversation was a one liner here or there that usually topped any other quip that came before it; there were never any lectures or words of reproach; he used just a few words to compliment my mother on that night's dinner: The best Yankee bean soup you ever made, Betty—but when he wasn't home, we missed him, for reasons words could not express.

BLACK, HARRY G.
  St. George Theatre                    1914

BLAKE, B. K.
  B. K. Blake, Inc.                     1912

BLANKENHORN, DAVID
  Cosmocolor Corp.                      1914

BLUMBERG, N. J.
  Universal Pictures                    1913

BLUMENTHAL, BEN
  Techs Corporation                     1911

BOND, CLAYTON E.
  Warner Bros. Theatres                 1907

BOWEN, JACK
  Loew's, Inc.                          1912

BRANDT, HARRY
  Brandt Theatres                       1914

BRANDT, WILLIAM
  Brandt Theatres                       1905

BRECHER, LEO                            1910

BRULATOUR, JULES E.                     1897

BUCKLEY, HARRY D.
  United Artists Corp.                  1913

BUXBAUM, HARRY H.
  Twentieth Century-Fox                 1913

CADORET, W. H.                          1909

CAHIL, FRANK E. JR.
  Warner Bros.                          1914

CAMMACK, BEN Y.
  RKO Radio Pictures (Dallas)           1916

## PURPOSE

**P**ICTURE PIONEERS, INC., was formed for the express purpose of bringing into closer contact, men who, for twenty-five years or more, have played a part in the development of the Motion Picture Industry. It was believed that these men, having much in common, would enjoy renewing old friendships. The gratifying growth of the organization is proof that the idea was sound. At the November 19th, 1942 Dinner, forty new members were inducted.

## WE ARE PROUD OF;

*Suzanne Freid and Lyla Blake, two of our Juniors. They registered with us in 1941 and both are now 16 years of age. They have given over 300 hours of service. That's a lot of hours when you figure they go to school 'til three o'clock and can only volunteer for a short time each day. Both girls have done clerical work in the office and have made scrapbooks to be sent to service men in hospitals. They have knitted squares to be used for afghans and have sewed together odd pieces of material for stuffed animals which are sent to children's nurseries. They have worked for the Victory Pastime Committee by packing Christmas boxes for service men. They have helped in the Victory Book Campaign by riding around in a gaily painted horsedrawn vehicle (of questionable vintage) to collect magazines and books from many apartments. Suzanne and Lyla are just two examples of what our Juniors can do.*

# Lyla Goes to War

It's not that I think we would have lost World War II if I hadn't done my bit—I'm just sayin'. . .

I was fourteen when I signed up with the AWVS, the American Women's Voluntary Services. My friend Suzy and I, an inseparable team, were assigned to the Junior Division. Two afternoons a week we collected tin foil and rolled it into balls—gigantic balls that would be recycled and used in parts for airplanes and other military equipment. Because our high school let out at one o'clock every day, in order to allow the army use of the building in the afternoon, we could work a full four hours, separating the foil from gum wrappers and cigarette packs, feeling terribly official in the snappy blue uniforms we were required (and happy) to wear when on the job or on parade.

Although the separation process was tedious, we were convinced it was of vital importance to the war effort. For all we knew, in some little corner somewhere on one of those B-17s roaring overhead, there was a Juicy Fruit wrapper that we, ourselves, had peeled. Talk about pride.

Working two days at the AWVS was very gratifying, but that still left us with three other days to give to our country. After much consideration, we decided to enter the labor market. So many men and women were in the armed services or working in factories, even high school students, who in other times might not have stood a chance, were sought after by employers. Feeling it was our patriotic duty to help out wherever we could, we answered an ad in a local paper for the position of kindergartner.

A nursery school on the East Side, close to Hunter, needed two girls to take a class of three- and four-year-olds to Central Park in the afternoon. We applied for the job—no references, no experience—and were hired on the spot. The fact that the pay was only a couple of dollars a day probably dissuaded older girls from applying. To us, that we were paid at all, just to take some tots to the park, was pretty exciting. We could hardly wait to begin.

As the youngest in the family, I had never been responsible for anyone younger than myself. The term "babysitting" had not even come into being yet, so when we arrived at the school the next day and were presented with ten or twelve little children who needed help getting their coats on, I began stuffing arms into armholes without regard to cries of pain or "I want my Mommy." I had been told to get six of them dressed; and by George, they were going to be dressed. I left no button unbuttoned.

Meanwhile, Suzy used a softer approach—she had a younger sister—and managed to get her six dressed and ready without any major incident, and when it came time for the tots to choose which one of us he or she would like to hold hands with, it was Suzy all the way. In fact, one little blonde, three year old, whose arm, unfortunately, had gotten stuck midway in her sleeve, looked up at me with steely blue eyes and announced for all to hear: "I don't like you." Deeply hurt, but determined to carry on, I continued herding the others into a manageable line, and off we went. Our employment lasted only a few weeks, until one of the parents found out her child was being taken to the park with eleven others in the questionable custody of two fourteen-year-old girls.

Undaunted, I was determined to put all I had into winning the war, and one of the things I had was my sister, who was old enough to join the WACs but to my great frustration had not shown any inclination to fight with anyone other than me. At fourteen or fifteen, I was still too young to volunteer; she, on the other hand, at nineteen or twenty, was the perfect candidate. Because she preferred walking into the Stagedoor Canteen (she was going to be an actress and went to The American Academy of Dramatic Arts) to walking into a recruitment center, I did it for her. Somehow, I'm not sure how I managed it, I convinced a WAC in the Army recruitment office to come to our apartment and talk to my sister. Imagine my mother's surprise when she answered the door and found a recruitment officer, in full uniform, asking if she was the mother of June Blake, and if June was at home. Lucky for me she was not, and after a long discussion, in which my mother tried to convince me winning the war was not completely my responsibility, I let June off the hook—but only after she agreed to at least read the material the officer had left.

In 1944, the war was entering its third year, and I was entering my sixteenth. I could finally do more toward the war effort than collect tin foil. I was old enough now, by our family's standards, to date, and how better to serve my country than to accept the invitation from Mrs. Kramer's son, home on furlough, to go roller skating at Gay Blades or Mrs. Cohn's son, just back from overseas, to go to the Paramount to see Frank Sinatra? This was the least I could do for our returning heroes.

As it happens, dating servicemen or former servicemen worked out well for me. In 1946, when Mrs. Ward, another friend of my mother's, asked if I would like to meet her son, Rusty, an Air Force sergeant who was returning that month from Burma, I dutifully agreed, and five years later, yadda yadda yadda— we were married. End of story.

# In Closing---

⁊

The trouble with leaving a neighborhood like the Upper
West Side where you were born and grew up is—only
you remember you ever lived there. Even if P.S. 54 were
still standing, it's not likely I could find the desk I sat at
in third grade, despite the fact that Billy Cushman
carved a little heart in it with my initials, "LHB," in the
middle (I never knew how he found out my middle
name was Harriet), alongside the other carvings of the
ages. And though you hear of people going back to visit
the house in which they were born in Yonkers or Scars-
dale, if I were to ring the doorbell at Apartment 4A at
245 West 104th Street, having somehow gotten past the
doorman, I'm not sure the present occupant, now an
owner, would let me in to see if the lights were still
flashing into "my" bedroom from the sign across the
street.

Cities are not sentimental. The UWS has new
children now—and I suspect never even thinks about
Her oldest offspring, those of us who danced around
the Maypole in Central Park on the First of May each
year, or waved and received the royal wave in return
from King George VI and his Queen, Elizabeth, as they
drove by in their long, open touring car—he with a
chestful of heraldic medals; she dressed in heavenly
blue from her softly turned hat to the tips of her toes.

We were the ones who watched our beloved
streetcars disappear from Broadway, replaced by ordinary buses like those that serviced most of the other

avenues in the city. We walked beneath the El on Columbus Avenue and rode the #5 Fifth Avenue double-decker buses we boarded on Riverside Drive.

Wherever I have gone in later life, I have taken "the neighborhood" with me. When I moved out of the city, I almost felt my description should be hyphenated: Lyla Ward—a New York-Connecticut Yankee.

Anyone who says and believes that "There's no going home again" has never written a memoir. In writing about the neighborhood where I grew up, I did find my way home again without too much difficulty—but maybe that's because a good part of me never left.

Chicago Tribune

SECTION
2

# PERSPECTIVE

SUNDAY
DECEMBER 9, 2007

A WEEKLY JOURNAL OF COMMENTARY, ANALYSIS AND OPINION

## A HEBREW SCHOOL LESSON HITS HOME

# Keeping The Peace, and The Tree, at Christmas

Our mistake was sending our children to Hebrew school.

But how were we to know that once a girl has worn Queen Esther's crown in a Purim festival, she is less likely to accept the pluralistic philosophy of her parents? Nor could we have known how seductive the power of Hanukkah would prove. Eight nights of presents and the best kind of Jewish gelt: chocolate!

There we were, leaving cookies and milk out for Santa and hearing our own flesh and blood scold us sternly: "Christmas is really not our holiday!" So why did we do it? Why did we send our two little girls out from a happy, non-observant Jewish home to a place that filled their heads with doubt and caused them ultimately to ask the dreaded question: Why do we have a Christmas tree?

Simple. We sent them to Hebrew school because we wanted to do the right thing.

This was back in the '60s, and we were living in a religiously diverse neighborhood of Catholics, Protestants and a few Jewish families, in Stamford, Conn. We decided it would be better for our daughters if they learned something about their ancestors' history.

Home schooling was not an option. I had never gone to Hebrew school. Every year I struggled to remember, "Why on this day [Passover], do we [forgo Arnold's multi-grain light and] eat matzo?" And tell me again, who was Elijah?

My husband, on the other hand, was a bar mitzvah boy, God-fearing and well-informed. But he grew to have little patience for organized religion.

Our children's friends either attended parochial schools, studied catechism after school or went to religious classes on Saturday or Sunday.

Being people of moderate temperament, neither vehemently for or against religious education, and loving parents who did not want to risk our daughters' having to grapple with religious insecurity later in life, we took the plunge and joined the reform temple.

That's when our troubles began.

By the time our older daughter was in 3rd grade, she had learned the phrase "mixed message" and how to apply it. By 4th grade, she would accuse us of "betraying our people."

Her sister, whose teacher that year had denounced "those Jews who celebrated the birth of Christ by putting up trees in his honor," would insist that the Christmas tree go. The presents, she allowed, were not so traitorous.

Attacked by our very own children, for whom my husband had spent many a Christmas Eve (sometimes into the morning) putting together swing sets and model kitchens and Barbie Dream Houses, we found ourselves having to defend our feelings about the holiday.

We didn't think that by celebrating Christmas we were in any way denying our roots. We pointed out that the Christmas tree, after all, was a pagan custom, a symbol of fertility adopted by Christians to represent rebirth. It really had nothing to do with Christ, especially if decorated with non-religious items. And angels never adorned our branches.

So why was it wrong to celebrate this happy, festive, American (as we saw it) holiday?

Having grown up in the 1930s and '40s in a New York neighborhood that was probably 95 percent Jewish, I had never been confused about my identity. All my friends were Jewish. We prided ourselves on taking matzo sandwiches to school during Passover. My grandmother wore white on Yom Kippur. And when we sang "Silent Night" in Public School 54, I carefully "mmm-mmed" over the "Christ our Savior" part and picked up again at "is born." The name "Jesus" never crossed my lips. He was not a part of our Christmas.

The holiday season was called the Christmas season then, and nobody I knew "celebrated" Hanukkah. I don't remember seeing a menorah glowing in any apartment window, but looking up and down the avenue at Christmas time, one could see Christmas-tree lights twinkling in the windows of apartment after apartment.

The first Christmas I remember did not include a tree. My brother set up electric trains to circle a card table, and we put our gifts in the center of the table. In the morning, he would throw the switch, and the trains would run maniacally around the tracks, hooting and whistling as we pulled out our gifts.

This went on for a few years until my brother was old enough — and had a dollar of his own — to buy a small tree that fit on the card table, where we continued to put our carefully wrapped packages.

The tree grew larger year by year until it no longer fit on the table, and by the time I was a teenager, it was man-size and stood, in all its over-trimmed majesty, in front of our (nonwood- burning) fireplace.

The rebellion we faced decades later from our own children was easy to resolve, without having to abandon the Christmas tree. We certainly were not anti-Hanukkah, so once our girls had had their religious awakening, we had no trouble throwing ourselves wholeheartedly into this additional season. We lit the candles, said the prayers, sang "The Dreidel Song" and gave small gifts on each of the eight nights.

Hanukkah was established as a mild tradition in our family. And even after our daughters started celebrating it in their own homes, my husband and I continued to put the shamas in its place each night. We would light the little menorah, bought years ago in the temple gift shop, and sometimes sing the first few lines, really the only ones we knew, of "The Dreidel Song." But on Christmas Eve, mixed message intact, my husband and I still trim our tree, card-table size once again. The blue and white lights twinkle, and a non-sectarian snowflake serves as our topper.

Then while Bing Crosby sings in the background, we begin our familiar celebration, guilt- free and looking forward to opening our presents in the morning.

*"Originally published in the Chicago Tribune on Dec. 9, 2007. Reprinted by permission."*

# Gray Matter

The first gray hair you hardly see,
The second one you hide,
The third is still a novelty,
A cinch to brush aside,
But then the snow starts making
    tracks,
With new streaks every day,
And you are forced to face the facts:
You're prematurely gray.

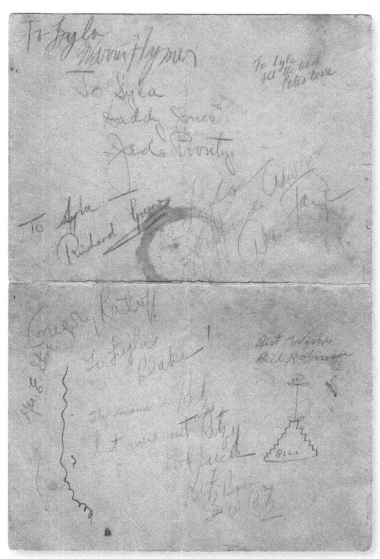

*Autographs on the back of a Twentieth Century Fox*
*Commissary menu my father brought back for me from*
*Hollywood—Bill Robinson drew the little staircase on*
*the lower right to commemorate the historic dance he*
*did with Shirley Temple in "The Little Colonel" 1935.*
*Other stars of the day added their well wishes—*
*Richard Green, Jed Prouty ("Daddy Jones"), Peter Lorre,*
*Gregory Ratoff, and the three Ritz Brothers—*
*"Our name is Ritz, but we're not Ritzy"—*

*Lila Lee: The silent movie star whose first name I bear—Her nickname "Cuddles," given to her as a child when she appeared in Gus Edward's Kiddie Review, remained with her as she emerged as a star playing opposite some of the leading matinee idols of the time—Conrad Nagel, Wallace Reid and Rudolph Valentino.*

In the 1920's, my Riverside Theater at 96th Street and Broadway was B. F. Keith's Riverside and featured some of the leading vaudevillians of the day. Gus Edwards , star of this show , presented new talent in his Protégé Week.

*Broadway, Schrafft's and Seeded Rye*

*Me with actors, Leo Genn and Mark Stevens
on a trip to Hollywood in 1944*

# Acknowledgements

My deepest thanks to everyone who has offered help and support in bringing this project to fruition, in particular, *Carol Gaskin*, a skilled and patient editor, who from the very beginning saw my loosely collected essays as a book; *Annette Bensen*, book designer extraordinaire, who with unflappable dedication, designed the very book I had in mind;--- the *West Side Rag*, and editor, *Avi*, whose lively stories rekindled my interest in the past and present of the Upper West Side; *Donica O'Bradovich*, creator and co-admin. with Ruben Iglesias of the Facebook group, "*Growing Up on The Old Upper West Side*," and all the members who continue to discover and pass along images and comments about a time and place we shared, and---

Thanks to all those fellow Upper West Siders who have taken the time to write or call or reminisce over a cup of tea: *Mary Ellen Siegel*, *Edith Katz*, *Alice Levine*, *Rochelle Steiner*, *Steve Fox*, *Amanda Nash*, *Carol Fradkin Bright*, *Elaine Wallach Sclar*, *Fred Rosenberg*, *Jen Rubin*, *Harriet Spina*, *Sally Sacks*, *Howard Freeman*, *Johanna Damgaard Liander*, *John Pressman*, *Joyce Hunt*, *Tim Gavigan*, *Linda Weiss*, *Margaret Ryan*, *Mark Korman*, *Roz Rosenbluth*, *Peter Berk*, *Lee Apt*, *Alice Simpson*, and a special thanks to *Joanne Hamburger* for sharing her grandfather, *Harry J. Oshiver's* painting, "*Boys Playing Marbles*," with us.

# Photo Credits

Thank you to the following people and institutions for digitizing your photo collections and allowing me the use of these wonderful vintage images to illustrate my essays.

*Camel sign*—Library of Congress; *"Floating Bath" in Hudson River*-- New York City Parks Photo Archive; *P.S. 54, 104th Street and Amsterdam Avenue*-- Millstein Division of United States History, Local History and Genealogy, the New York Public Library, Astor, Lenox and Tilden Foundation; *Old Schoolroom*—permission Arcangel Images, Inc., Photographer—Jill Battaglia; *East River Savings Bank, 96th Street and Amsterdam Avenue*-- Millstein Division of United States History, Local History and Genealogy, the New York Public Library, Astor, Lenox and Tilden Foundation; *Trousseaux Monograms*— Photographer, Sue Shea; *The Middle, 1937*—Photo by Percy Loomis Sperr ©Milstein Division, The New York Public Library; *Broadway Before The Middle, 1906*—Milstein Division of United States History, Local History & Genealogy, The New York Public Library, Astor, Lenox and Tilden Foundations; *82nd Street Schrafft's and Schrafft's interior*—Library of Congress

**Lyla Blake Ward**'s writing career officially began in 1949, when she sold her first poem to Collier's magazine:

## Betrayal at Plymouth
Greasy gizzards, flying feathers
Oh the difference it would make,
If the Pilgrims had decided
To give thanks with sirloin steak.

Over the past 65 years, numerous magazines and newspapers have published her work. Humorous verse, op-eds, personal essays and social commentary have appeared in *Good Housekeeping*, *The Wall Street Journal*, *Cosmopolitan*, *Woman's Day*, *Family Circle*, *the Washington Post*, *the Chicago Tribune*, *the Christian Science Monitor* and *Newsday*, among many others.

Her first book, *How to Succeed at Aging without Really Dying*, a collection of humorous essays published in 2010, appeared on Amazon's 2011 list of the Top 100 Books. and was published in Germany under the title: Wo Ist Meine Lesebrille (Where Are My Reading Glasses?)

Residing in Somers, New York, with Russ, her husband of 64 years, Ward enjoys reading, wrestling with crossword puzzles and Double Crostics, baking, knitting, crocheting, and watching endless reruns of "Seinfeld."

**BROADWAY**

**SCHRAFFT'S**

**and Seeded Rye**

Growing Up Slightly Jewish
on the Upper West Side

In *Broadway, Schrafft's and Seeded Rye—
Growing Up Slightly Jewish on the Upper West Side,*
Lyla Blake Ward, author of How to Succeed at
Aging Without Really Dying, tells it like it was,
growing up on the Upper West Side of
Manhattan in the 1930's and early 1940's.
Through essays and poems, histories and vintage
photos, Ward makes this unique neighborhood--
72nd street to 110th-- east and west of
Broadway, come alive.

Looking back-- and back---and back, she is able
to recapture the atmosphere of this singular
community, its culture and the families who lived
there--a place, according to the author, where
almost everyone she knew was Jewish and only
the pigeons ate white bread.